DROPSHIPPING SHOPIFY FOR BEGINNERS

The All-Inclusive Guide to Establishing and Running a Booming Dropshipping Business

T.M.T HARRISON

TABLE OF CONTENTS

INTRODUCTION

Starting your own online business can feel like diving into a vast ocean. The possibilities are endless, but the challenges can be just as immense. You might be dreaming of financial independence, a flexible schedule, or simply the thrill of building something from scratch. Whatever your motivation, you've taken a pivotal step by considering dropshipping with Shopify. This introduction is intended to be your compass, guiding you through the early stages of your e-commerce journey.

What is Dropshipping?

Dropshipping is a retail fulfillment method where you, as the seller, don't keep products in stock. Instead, when a customer orders a product from your store, you purchase the item from a third-party supplier who then ships it directly to the customer. You act as the middleman, handling the marketing and sales while the supplier takes care of the inventory and shipping.

Key Features of Dropshipping:

1. No Inventory Management: One of the biggest advantages of dropshipping is that you don't need to worry about stocking or managing inventory. This eliminates the risk of overstocking or running out of stock and reduces the need for storage space.

2. *Lower Upfront Costs:* Traditional retail businesses require significant upfront investment in inventory. Dropshipping allows you to start your business with minimal financial investment because you only purchase products after a customer has placed an order.

3. *Flexibility and Scalability:* Dropshipping provides the flexibility to operate your business from anywhere in the world. You can manage your store from anywhere with an internet connection. It's also easy to scale your business by adding new products without the need for additional inventory management.

4. *Wide Product Selection:* Since you don't have to pre-purchase inventory, you can offer a wide variety of products to your customers. This allows you to test different products and niches to find what sells best without significant financial risk.

5. *Time Efficiency:* Since you're outsourcing inventory management and order fulfillment to suppliers, you save a significant amount of time. This allows you to focus on marketing, customer service, and other activities that drive business growth.

Dropshipping, like any other business strategy, is not without its obstacles. These include lower profit margins compared to traditional retail, reliance on suppliers for product quality and shipping times, and the need for effective marketing strategies to stand out in a competitive market. But don't worry, this guide will address these challenges and provide you with strategies to overcome them.

Why Choose Shopify?

When it comes to building a dropshipping business, choosing the right e-commerce platform is crucial. Shopify is one of the most popular and user-friendly platforms available, making it an excellent choice for beginners and seasoned entrepreneurs alike. Here's why Shopify stands out as the ideal platform for your dropshipping venture:

User-Friendly Interface:

Shopify's intuitive interface makes it easy for you to set up and manage your online store, even if you have no prior experience with web design or e-commerce. The platform is designed to be user-friendly, allowing you to focus on growing your business rather than getting bogged down by technical details.

Extensive App Store:

Shopify offers a vast array of apps and integrations that can enhance your store's functionality. Whether you need tools for marketing, inventory management, customer service, or analytics, Shopify's app store has you covered. Many of these apps are specifically designed to support dropshipping, making it easier to find and manage suppliers, automate order processing, and optimize your store's performance.

Built-In Payment Processing:

Shopify provides a seamless payment processing system, allowing you to accept payments from customers through various methods, including credit cards, PayPal, and other popular gateways. This built-in functionality ensures that your customers have a smooth and secure checkout experience.

Reliable Hosting and Security:

With Shopify, you don't need to worry about hosting or security issues. The platform handles all the technical aspects of running an online store, including server maintenance, security updates, and backups. This means your store will be fast, reliable, and secure, providing a positive shopping experience for your customers.

Customizable Themes:

Shopify offers a wide range of professionally designed themes that you can customize to match your brand's aesthetic. Whether you prefer a minimalist look or a vibrant, colorful design, you'll find a theme that suits your style. Customizing your store's appearance is straightforward, thanks to Shopify's drag-and-drop editor and extensive documentation.

Excellent Customer Support:

Shopify's customer support team is available 24/7 to assist you with any issues or questions you might have. Whether you need help setting up your store, troubleshooting technical problems, or optimizing your site for better performance, Shopify's support team is there to help you every step of the way.

Community and Resources:

Shopify boasts a large and active community of users, developers, and experts who share their knowledge and experiences. You'll find forums, blogs, webinars, and tutorials that provide valuable insights and tips for running a successful dropshipping business. This wealth of resources ensures that you're never alone on your entrepreneurial journey.

HOW THIS GUIDE WILL HELP YOU SUCCEED.

Embarking on a dropshipping journey can be both exciting and daunting. There's a lot to learn, from setting up your store and sourcing products to marketing and managing customer relationships. This guide is designed to be your comprehensive companion, providing you with step-by-step instructions, practical tips, and expert advice to help you build and grow a successful dropshipping business using Shopify.

What You Will Learn:

1. Understanding Dropshipping: We'll start with the basics of dropshipping, including how it works, its advantages and challenges, and how to choose the right niche for your business. By the end of this section, you'll have a strong base from which to grow.

2. *Setting up Your Shopify Store:* We'll walk you through the process of setting up your Shopify store, from creating an account to designing your storefront. You'll learn how to choose and customize a theme, add products, and set up essential features like payment gateways and shipping options.

3. *Sourcing Products and Suppliers:* Finding reliable suppliers is crucial for the success of your dropshipping business. We'll explore different sourcing methods, including using dropshipping platforms, reaching out to manufacturers, and attending trade shows. You'll learn how to evaluate suppliers, negotiate terms, and build strong relationships.

4. *Managing Your Store:* Running a dropshipping business involves more than just setting up a store and sourcing products. We'll cover important aspects of store management, including inventory management, order fulfillment, and customer service. You'll learn how to automate processes to save time and ensure a smooth operation.

5. *Marketing and Driving Traffic:* Attracting customers to your store is essential for generating sales. We'll dive into various marketing strategies, including search engine optimization (SEO), social media marketing, email marketing, and paid advertising. You'll discover how to create compelling content, engage with your audience, and drive targeted traffic to your store.

6. *Optimizing for Success:* Continuous improvement is key to long-term success. We'll show you how to analyze your store's performance using analytics tools, identify areas for improvement, and implement changes to boost conversions and sales. You'll learn how to scale your business, expand your product line, and increase profitability.

7. *Legal and Financial Considerations:* Understanding the legal and financial aspects of running a dropshipping business is crucial for compliance and sustainability. We'll cover topics such as setting up a business entity, tax obligations, and financial management. You'll learn how to protect your business and ensure financial stability.

OUR APPROACH

This guide is designed to be practical, actionable, and easy to follow. We've broken down complex concepts into simple, step-by-step instructions, and provided real-world examples to illustrate key points. Our goal is to make the learning process enjoyable and engaging, so you feel confident and empowered as you embark on your dropshipping journey.

We also recognize that every entrepreneur's journey is unique. That's why we've included tips and advice for different scenarios, whether you're starting with a small budget, targeting a specific niche, or aiming for rapid growth. This guide is flexible and adaptable, allowing you to tailor the strategies to your specific needs and goals.

RESOURCES AND TOOLS

In addition to the comprehensive content in this guide, we have included a list of valuable resources and tools to support your dropshipping business. You will find recommended apps, software, and services that can streamline your operations, enhance your marketing efforts, and improve your overall efficiency.

We have also provided a glossary of common e-commerce and dropshipping terms to help you navigate the jargon and technical language you might encounter along the way. This glossary will be a handy reference as you dive deeper into the world of dropshipping.

ENCOURAGEMENT AND SUPPORT

Starting a dropshipping business is a significant undertaking, but you don't have to do it alone. This guide is here to support you every step of the way, offering encouragement, practical advice, and a sense of community. Remember, every successful dropshipping entrepreneur started where you are now—taking that first step towards building a business and a brighter future.

As you work through this guide, keep an open mind and be prepared to learn and adapt. E-commerce is a dynamic field, and staying flexible and resilient will serve you well.

Celebrate your accomplishments, learn from your mistakes, and keep pushing forward. With dedication, perseverance, and the right guidance, you have the potential to achieve great things in the world of dropshipping.

CONCLUSION

We're thrilled to have you join us on this journey into the exciting world of dropshipping with Shopify. This guide is your roadmap to building a successful and sustainable business, providing you with the knowledge, tools, and confidence you need to succeed. So, let's get started!

Flip the page, get started, and embark on a dropshipping journey. Your dreams of being an entrepreneur are attainable, and we are here to support you in turning them into reality.

CHAPTER ONE
The Basics of Dropshipping

Dropshipping is a retail fulfillment method that allows you to run an online store without ever holding inventory. Instead of purchasing products in bulk and storing them, you partner with suppliers who handle the inventory and shipping for you. Here's how it works:

1. Setting up Your Online Store: You create an online store using a platform like Shopify. This is where customers will browse and purchase products.

2. Listing Products: You list products on your store that you source from third-party suppliers. These products can range from electronics and clothing to niche items like handmade crafts or eco-friendly goods.

3. Customer Orders: When a customer places an order on your store, you receive the order details and payment.

4. Order Fulfillment: You forward the order details to your supplier, who then prepares and ships the product directly to the customer.

5. Profit: The difference between the price you charge the customer and the price you pay the supplier is your profit.

This model is popular among entrepreneurs because it minimizes upfront investment and simplifies the logistics of running an e-commerce business.

How Dropshipping Works

To better understand dropshipping, here's a breakdown of the process step-by-step:

1. Choosing a Niche:

Choosing the right niche is critical to your dropshipping success. A niche is a specific segment of the market sector that you want to target with your products. Instead of trying to sell everything to everyone, focusing on a niche allows you to cater to a specific audience, making your marketing efforts more effective.

2. Finding Reliable Suppliers:

Suppliers are the backbone of your dropshipping business. They provide the products you sell and handle the shipping. It's important to choose reputable suppliers to ensure product quality and timely delivery.

3. Setting Up Your Shopify Store:

Creating a professional and user-friendly online store is essential for attracting, converting and retaining customers. Shopify's platform makes it easy to set up your store, customize it to reflect your brand, and manage day-to-day operations.

4. Marketing Your Store:

Once your store is set up, the next step is to attract customers. Effective marketing strategies will help you drive traffic to your store and convert visitors into buyers.

5. Managing Orders and Customer Service:

Efficient order management and excellent customer service are vital for maintaining customer satisfaction and loyalty.

Challenges of Dropshipping

1. Lower Profit Margins:

While dropshipping reduces upfront costs, the trade-off is lower profit margins compared to traditional retail. Since you're buying products individually from suppliers, you don't benefit from bulk purchasing discounts. Additionally, you'll need to account for marketing and advertising expenses, which can further eat into your profits.

2. Reliance on Suppliers:

Your business heavily depends on the reliability of your suppliers. If a supplier fails to deliver products on time, sends incorrect items, or runs out of stock, it directly affects your customers and your reputation. Building strong relationships with trustworthy suppliers is crucial for mitigating this risk.

3. Limited Control over Quality and Shipping:

Since you don't handle the products yourself, you have limited control over their quality and the shipping process. Poor product quality or delayed shipments can lead to customer dissatisfaction and negative reviews. To minimize these issues, it's essential to vet suppliers thoroughly and communicate your expectations clearly.

4. High Competition:

Dropshipping has become a popular business model, leading to increased competition in many niches. Standing out in a crowded market requires effective marketing strategies, unique branding, and excellent customer service. Finding a profitable niche with lower competition can also give you an edge.

5. Customer Service Challenges:

As the intermediary between your customers and suppliers, you'll need to manage customer inquiries, complaints, and returns. Providing excellent customer service can be challenging when you have limited control over the product and shipping. However, clear communication and prompt responses can help build trust and loyalty.

In conclusion, Dropshipping offers an accessible and flexible way to start an online business, with numerous benefits like low startup costs, no inventory management, and the ability to offer a wide range of products. However, it also comes with challenges such as lower profit margins, reliance on suppliers, and high competition.

Choosing Your Niche

Choosing your niche is the foundation of your business, it sets the stage for everything that follows. Let's explore why selecting the right niche is crucial and how you can research and choose a profitable niche that aligns with your interests and market demand.

The Importance of Niche Selection

Choosing the right niche is like finding the perfect plot of land for your house. It determines the potential success and growth of your business. Here are some key reasons why niche selection is vital:

1. *Targeted Marketing:* A well-defined niche allows you to tailor your marketing efforts to a specific audience. This focused approach makes your marketing more effective and efficient, as you can speak directly to the needs and desires of your potential customers.

2. *Reduced Competition:* While some niches are highly competitive, others may have less competition, giving you a better chance to stand out. By identifying a niche with lower competition, you can carve out a unique space for your business.

3. *Customer Loyalty:* When you cater to a specific niche, you can build stronger relationships with your customers. They are more likely to become loyal, repeat buyers because they feel understood and valued.

4. *Higher Conversion Rates:* Targeting a niche market means you're speaking directly to people who are interested in what you offer. This relevance can lead to higher conversion rates, as your products and marketing messages resonate more deeply with your audience.

5. Brand Authority: Specializing in a niche can help you establish your brand as an authority in that field. When customers see you as an expert, they are more likely to trust you and purchase from you.

How to Research and Choose a Profitable Niche

Now that we understand the importance of niche selection, let's dive into the process of researching and choosing a profitable niche for your dropshipping business. Here's a step-by-step guide to help get started:

1. Identify Your Interests and Passions:

Start by brainstorming niches that align with your interests, hobbies, and passions. Running a business requires dedication and effort, so choosing a niche you're passionate about can keep you motivated. Make a list of topics or industries that excite you. This initial list doesn't have to be perfect; it's just a starting point.

2. Evaluate Market Demand:

Once you have a list of potential niches, it's time to evaluate the market demand for each one. You want to choose a niche that has a significant number of people interested in it. Here are some tools and methods to assess market demand:

- Google Trends: Use Google Trends to see the search volume and trends for your niche keywords over time. This tool can help you identify whether interest in your niche is growing, stable, or declining.

- Keyword Research: Use keyword research tools like Ahrefs, SEMrush, or Google Keyword Planner to find popular keywords related to your niche. Search for keywords with a high search volume and minimal competition.

- Amazon Best Sellers: Browse Amazon's best sellers list in different categories to see what products are popular. This can give you insights into trending niches and product ideas.

- Social Media: Check social media platforms like Instagram, Pinterest, and Facebook to see what topics and products are trending. Look for communities and influencers within your potential niches to gauge interest levels.

3. Analyze the Competition:

While you want to find a niche with demand, it's also important to assess the level of competition. When there is too much competition, it can be difficult to stand out.

Finding Trustworthy Suppliers and Sources for High-Quality Products

Now that you have a clear direction, it's time to go into the next crucial aspect of your dropshipping business: finding reliable suppliers and sourcing high-quality products. This section will guide you through the process of identifying and partnering with suppliers who can provide you with the best products for your store.

Why Supplier Selection Matters

Selecting the right suppliers is vital for several reasons:

1. Product Quality: High-quality products lead to satisfied customers, fewer returns, and positive reviews, which can enhance your brand's reputation.

2. Consistency: Reliable suppliers ensure a steady supply of products, helping you maintain inventory levels and meet customer demand.

3. Shipping and Delivery: Efficient and timely shipping improves customer satisfaction and reduces the likelihood of disputes and refunds.

4. Pricing and Margins: Competitive pricing from suppliers can improve your profit margins and allow you to offer competitive prices to your customers.

5. Communication and Support: Good suppliers are responsive and provide excellent customer support, which is crucial for resolving any issues that may arise.

Types of Suppliers

Before we go into finding suppliers, it's essential to understand the different types of suppliers you might encounter:

1. Manufacturers: These are the companies that produce the products. Working directly with manufacturers can offer you the best prices but may require larger order quantities.

2. Wholesalers: Wholesalers purchase products in bulk from manufacturers and sell them in smaller quantities. They are suitable for dropshippers who don't need to order in large quantities.

3. Dropshipping Suppliers: These suppliers specialize in dropshipping and handle the storage, packaging, and shipping of products directly to your customers.

How to Find Reliable Suppliers

Finding the right suppliers involves research, vetting, and sometimes a bit of trial and error. Here are a few steps to help you identify trustworthy suppliers:

1. Research Online Marketplaces:

Online marketplaces like AliExpress, Oberlo, and Alibaba are popular platforms for finding dropshipping suppliers. These platforms offer a wide range of products and suppliers, making it easy to find items that fit your niche.

- AliExpress: Known for its vast selection of products and competitive prices, AliExpress is a favorite among dropshippers. You can browse products, read reviews, and evaluate supplier ratings.

- **Oberlo:** Oberlo integrates directly with Shopify, making it seamless to import products into your store. It provides tools to find and manage dropshipping suppliers.

- **Alibaba:** While Alibaba is geared more towards bulk orders, it's still a valuable resource for finding manufacturers and wholesalers. You can negotiate directly with suppliers for better pricing.

2. Use Supplier Directories:

Supplier directories list verified suppliers, making it easier to find reliable partners. Some popular directories include:

- **SaleHoo:** SaleHoo offers a directory of over 8,000 verified suppliers. It's a paid service, but it provides access to reliable suppliers and valuable market research tools.

- **Worldwide Brands:** This directory features certified wholesalers and dropshipping suppliers. It requires a one-time membership fee but offers access to high-quality suppliers.

- **Doba:** Doba aggregates suppliers and allows you to manage your dropshipping products from one platform. It's a subscription-based service with a wide range of products.

3. Attend Trade Shows and Networking Events:

Trade shows and industry events are excellent opportunities to meet suppliers in person. Building relationships with suppliers at these events can lead to better deals and long-term partnerships. Look for trade shows relevant to your niche and attend them to connect with potential suppliers.

4. Conduct Online Searches:

A simple online search can yield a wealth of supplier options. Use keywords related to your niche, such as "niche + dropshipping supplier" or "niche + wholesale supplier." Be sure to vet these suppliers carefully, as not all results will be reliable.

5. Check Industry Forums and Communities:

Online forums and communities, such as Reddit, Shopify Community, and specialized dropshipping forums, can provide recommendations and reviews of suppliers. Engaging with these communities can give you insights into the experiences of other dropshippers.

Vetting Your Suppliers

Once you have a list of potential suppliers, it's crucial to vet them to ensure they meet your standards. Here's how to evaluate suppliers effectively:

1. Request Samples:

Before committing to a supplier, request product samples to assess the quality firsthand. This step is essential to ensure the products meet your expectations and are suitable for your customers.

2. Evaluate Communication:

Good communication is vital for a smooth partnership. Pay attention to how responsive and helpful the supplier is during your initial interactions. Prompt and clear communication is a positive indicator of their reliability.

3. Check Reviews and Ratings:

Look for reviews and ratings on platforms like AliExpress, Alibaba, and supplier directories. Reviews from other dropshippers can provide useful information about the supplier's dependability, product quality, and shipment times.

4. Assess Shipping and Delivery Times:

Timely delivery is crucial for customer satisfaction. Inquire about the supplier's shipping methods, delivery times, and any tracking options they offer. Make sure their shipments' times are consistent with your consumers' expectations.

5. Negotiate Terms:

Don't hesitate to negotiate terms with suppliers. Discuss pricing, minimum order quantities, payment terms, and return policies. Building a good relationship with your supplier can lead to better terms and discounts.

When going into dropshipping with Shopify, understanding how to effectively research and choose a niche is crucial for success. Here's a detailed exploration of the tools and techniques you can use:

Tools for Niche Research

1. Google Trends: Google Trends is a powerful tool to explore the popularity of search terms over time. Here's how you can leverage it:

- Identify Trends: Use Google Trends to see if interest in your potential niche is growing or declining.

- Compare Keywords: Compare different keywords related to your niche to understand which ones are trending.

2. Keyword Research Tools: Tools like Google Keyword Planner, Ubersuggest, or Semrush can help you discover relevant keywords and estimate search volumes:

- Search Volume: Look for keywords with high search volumes to gauge potential demand.

- Long-tail Keywords: Target specific, less competitive long-tail keywords for niche specificity.

3. Social Media Platforms: Platforms like Facebook, Instagram, and Pinterest offer insights into audience interests and engagement:

- Groups and Pages: Join relevant groups and pages to understand discussions and interests within your niche.

- Hashtags: Monitor hashtags related to your niche to gauge popularity and engagement levels.

4. Competitor Analysis Tools: Tools such as Ahrefs or SpyFu can help you analyze competitors in your niche:

- **Identify Competitors:** Research top competitors to understand their product offerings, pricing strategies, and customer engagement tactics.

- **Gap Analysis:** Identify gaps or underserved areas within your niche that you can capitalize on.

5. E-commerce Platforms and Marketplaces: Look into platforms like Amazon, eBay, and Etsy to:

- **Identify Bestsellers:** Look for top-selling products within your potential niche to validate demand.

- **Customer Reviews:** Read customer reviews to understand pain points and product preferences.

Techniques for Niche Research

1. Passion and Knowledge:

- **Follow Your Interests:** Choose a niche that aligns with your passions or knowledge to stay motivated and informed.

- **Solve Problems:** Identify common problems or pain points within your chosen niche that your products can address.

2. Target Audience Research:

- Create Buyer Personas: Develop complete profiles of your ideal customers, including their demographics, interests, and purchasing habits.

- Survey Potential Customers: Use surveys or interviews to gather insights directly from your target audience.

3. Keyword Research:

- Use Seed Keywords: Start with broad keywords related to your niche and then narrow down to more specific long-tail keywords.

- SEO Analysis: Analyze SEO difficulty and competition for your chosen keywords to assess ranking feasibility.

4. Evaluate Profitability:

- Profit Margin Analysis: Calculate potential profit margins for products within your niche, considering costs like shipping and advertising.

- Seasonal Trends: Consider seasonal variations and trends that could impact product demand and sales.

5. Test Your Ideas:

- Set Up a Landing Page: Create a simple landing page to gauge interest and collect email addresses from potential customers.

- *Run Small Ads:* Test product ideas with small-scale Facebook or Google ads to measure click-through rates and conversions.

Effective niche research is foundational to your success in dropshipping with Shopify. By utilizing the right tools and techniques, understanding your target audience, and validating demand, you can confidently choose a niche that aligns with your interests and has the potential for profitability. Stay proactive in monitoring trends and adapting your strategy as you gain insights into market dynamics and customer preferences. This approach will not only help you establish a strong foundation but also position you for sustainable growth in the competitive world of dropshipping.

CHAPTER TWO
Setting Up Your Shopify Store

Before you go into setting up your store, it's important to understand what Shopify offers and how it can benefit your dropshipping business.

What is Shopify?

Shopify is a popular e-commerce platform that allows you to create and manage your online store without needing to worry about technical details like hosting or web development. It provides all the tools and features you need to start selling products online efficiently.

Why Choose Shopify?

- User-Friendly Interface: Shopify's intuitive dashboard makes it easy for beginners to set up and manage their stores.

- Built-in Marketing Tools: Access to built-in tools like SEO optimization and social media integrations helps you reach more customers.

- Scalability: Shopify scales with your business, allowing you to add features and customize your store as you grow.

- 24/7 Support: Benefit from Shopify's customer support team, available round-the-clock to assist with any issues you encounter.

Creating Your Shopify Account

Step 1: Sign Up for Shopify

- Go to Shopify's official website and click on the "Get Started" button.

- To set up an account, enter your email address, password, and shop name.

- Fill in the required information, including your name, address, and phone number.

Step 2: Choose a Plan

- Shopify offers different pricing plans (Basic Shopify, Shopify, Advanced Shopify) with varying features and transaction fees.

- Choose the plan that best financial your budget and business needs. Start with the Basic Shopify plan and then upgrade as your business expands.

Step 3: Set Up Your Store

- Customize your store's URL (domain name) or use Shopify's free MyShopify.com domain.

- Complete the store setup wizard by entering details about your business, such as industry and product types.

Navigating the Shopify Dashboard

Once your account is set up, you'll land on the Shopify dashboard, your command center for managing your store.

Overview of the Dashboard

- *Home:* The main dashboard where you can view store analytics, sales, and visitor data at a glance.

- *Orders:* Manage orders, fulfillments, and customer communications.

- *Products:* Add, edit, and organize your products, including descriptions, prices, and inventory.

- *Customers:* Access and manage customer data, such contact information and order history.

- *Analytics:* Track sales trends, traffic sources, and other key metrics to understand your store's performance.

- *Marketing:* Run campaigns, create discounts, and integrate with social media platforms to promote your products.

Key Features and Tools

- ***Theme Customization:*** Choose from Shopify's selection of themes or customize your store's appearance using the theme editor.

- ***App Store:*** Explore Shopify's App Store to find additional tools and integrations to enhance your store's functionality.

- ***Settings:*** Configure payment gateways, shipping options, taxes, and other store settings to ensure smooth operations.

Tips for Success

- ***Optimize Your Store:*** Use SEO best practices to improve visibility on search engines and attract organic traffic.

- ***Mobile-Friendly Design:*** Ensure your store is mobile-responsive to provide a seamless shopping experience on all devices.

- ***Customer Support:*** Offer excellent customer service to build trust and loyalty among your customers.

- ***Monitor Analytics:*** Regularly review analytics to identify opportunities for growth and areas for improvement.

Setting up your Shopify store is an exciting first step towards building a successful dropshipping business. By following this steps and familiarizing yourself with Shopify's tools and features, you'll be well-equipped to create a professional online store that attracts customers and drives sales. Remember, the key to success lies in continuous learning, adapting to market trends, and providing exceptional customer experiences.

Designing Your Store

Whether you're a seasoned entrepreneur or just getting started, designing your store is a critical step in creating a compelling online presence. A well-designed store can attract customers, build trust, and ultimately drive sales. In this chapter, we'll guide you through the essential elements of store design, from choosing and customizing a theme to branding your store with logos, colors, and fonts, and finally creating a user-friendly navigation system.

Choosing and Customizing a Shopify Theme

The first step in designing your Shopify store is choosing the right theme. Shopify offers a wide range of free and paid themes, each with its unique features and styles. The theme you choose will set the tone for your entire store, so it's essential to pick one that aligns with your brand and product offerings.

1. Browsing Themes:

Start by exploring the Shopify Theme Store, where you'll find a variety of themes categorized by industry, layout style, and features. Take your time to browse through the options and preview how different themes look in action. Pay attention to themes that match the aesthetic and functionality you're aiming for. Remember, your theme should complement your products and create a seamless shopping experience for your customers.

2. Key Considerations When Choosing a Theme:

- **Industry Suitability:** Some themes are specifically designed for certain industries, such as fashion, electronics, or home decor. Choose a theme that fits your niche to ensure it includes the features and layouts that will showcase your products effectively.

- **Responsiveness:** In today's mobile-driven world, having a responsive theme is non-negotiable. Ensure the theme you choose looks great and functions well on all devices, including smartphones and tablets.

- **Customization Options:** Look for themes with a high level of customization. You'll want the flexibility to tweak colors, fonts, layouts, and other design elements to match your brand identity.

- **User Reviews and Ratings:** Check out the reviews and ratings of the themes you're interested in. Feedback from other users can provide valuable insights into the theme's performance and ease of use.

3. Customizing Your Theme:

Once you've chosen a theme, it's time to make it your own. Customization allows you to tailor the theme to your brand's unique style and personality. Here's how to get started:

 - *Accessing the Theme Editor:* From your Shopify admin dashboard, select "Online Store" and then "Themes." To use the theme editor, click the "Customize" button next to your chosen theme.

- *Editing Colors and Fonts:* Use the theme editor to change the color scheme and fonts to match your brand. Consistent colors and fonts help create a cohesive and professional look. Choose a color palette that reflects your brand's personality, and select fonts that are easy to read and align with your brand's voice.

- *Customizing Layouts:* Most themes come with pre-designed layouts for different pages, such as the homepage, product pages, and collections. Customize these layouts to highlight your best-selling products, showcase promotions, and guide customers through their shopping journey.

- *Adding and Rearranging Sections:* Shopify themes often include customizable sections that you can add, remove, or rearrange. Use these sections to feature testimonials, blog posts, image galleries, and other content that enhances the shopping experience.

- *Integrating Apps:* Shopify's App Store offers a plethora of apps that can enhance your theme's functionality. From product reviews and social media feeds to advanced search and email marketing, there's an app for almost everything. Integrate the apps that align with your store's needs and goals.

Branding Your Store: Logos, Colors, and Fonts.

Branding is a crucial aspect of your Shopify store's design. A strong brand identity helps you stand out from the competition, build trust with customers, and create a memorable shopping experience. In this section, we'll cover the essentials of branding, including creating a logo, choosing colors, and selecting fonts.

1. Creating a Logo:

Your logo is the visual identity of your brand. It's often the first thing customers notice, so it's important to make a strong impression. Here are some tips for developing an excellent logo:

 - *Simplicity:* A simple logo is easy to identify and remember. Avoid clutter and keep the design simple and uncomplicated.

- *Relevance:* Ensure your logo reflects your brand's personality and values. Consider using symbols or icons that are related to your industry or products.

- *Scalability:* Your logo should look phenomenal at any size, be it on a business card or a billboard. Make sure it's scalable and legible in different contexts.

- *Professional Design:* If you're not a designer, consider hiring a professional or using online logo design tools. A well-designed logo can make a significant difference in how your brand is perceived.

2. Choosing Colors:

Colors play a vital role in conveying your brand's identity and evoking emotions. Here's how to choose a color palette for your store:

- *Brand Personality:* Think about the emotions and values you want your brand to convey. For example, blue often represents trust and reliability, while red can evoke excitement and energy.

- *Consistency:* Use your chosen colors consistently across all elements of your store, including the logo, website, social media, and marketing materials. Consistency helps build brand recognition.

- *Contrast:* Ensure there's enough contrast between your background and text colors to make your content easy to read. Use color contrast tools to check for accessibility.

- *Accent Colors:* Choose one or two accent colors to highlight important elements, such as call-to-action buttons and promotions. Accent colors can draw attention and guide customers' actions.

3. Selecting Fonts:

Fonts also contribute to your brand's personality and readability. Follow these guidelines when selecting fonts:

- **Readability:** Select fonts that are easy to read, particularly for body text. Avoid overly decorative fonts that can be difficult to understand.

- **Pairing Fonts:** Use a combination of fonts for different purposes. Typically, you'll want one font for headings and another for body text. Ensure the fonts complement each other and create a harmonious look.

- **Brand Voice:** Your font choices should align with your brand's voice. For example, a playful brand might use a more whimsical font, while a professional brand might opt for a classic, serif font.

- **Web-Safe Fonts:** Ensure your fonts are web-safe and compatible across different devices and browsers. Google Fonts is an excellent resource for finding web-safe fonts.

Creating a User-Friendly Navigation

A well-designed navigation system is essential for providing a smooth and enjoyable shopping experience. Effective navigation helps customers find what they're looking for quickly and easily, reducing frustration and increasing the likelihood of a purchase. Let's explore how to create a user-friendly navigation system for your Shopify store.

1. Organizing Your Menu:

Your store's menu is the primary way customers will navigate your site. Here are some tips for organizing it effectively:

- *Clear Categories:* Group your products into clear, logical categories. Avoid overwhelming customers with too many options. Aim for simplicity and clarity.

- *Dropdown Menus:* Use dropdown menus to organize subcategories and keep your main menu clean. Dropdowns allow customers to drill down into specific sections without cluttering the main navigation bar.

- *Priority Placement:* Place the most important and frequently visited categories at the top of your menu. Consider using analytics to determine which pages receive the most traffic and adjust your menu accordingly.

2. Creating a Search Function:

A search function is a must-have feature for any online store. It allows customers to find specific products quickly, especially if they have something particular in mind. Here's how to optimize your search function:

- *Visible Search Bar:* Ensure the search bar is prominently displayed on your homepage and other key pages. It should be easy to recognize and use.

- *Autocomplete:* Implement an autocomplete feature that suggests products as customers type. This can speed up the search process and help customers discover products they might not have considered.

- *Filters and Sorting:* Allow customers to filter search results by various criteria, such as price, popularity, and ratings. Sorting options help customers narrow down their choices and find what they're looking for more efficiently.

3. Utilizing Breadcrumbs:

Breadcrumbs are a secondary navigation aid that shows customers their location within your store's hierarchy. They provide a trail of links that lead back to previous pages, making it easy for customers to navigate back to higher-level categories. Here's how to use breadcrumbs effectively:

- *Visibility:* Place breadcrumbs at the top of your pages, just below the main menu. They should be easy to see and use.

- *Clarity:* Ensure the breadcrumb trail accurately reflects the structure of your site. Use clear and concise labels for each level.

- *Consistent Design:* Maintain a consistent design for breadcrumbs across all pages. This helps customers recognize and use them effectively.

4. Implementing a Footer Menu:

The footer menu is another important navigation element that can enhance the user experience. It typically includes links to essential pages and resources, such as:

- *Contact Information:* Provide easy access to your contact details, including email, phone number, and physical address.

- Customer Service: Include links to customer service pages, such as FAQs, shipping information, returns policy, and privacy policy.

- Social Media Links: Add icons and links to your social media profiles. This encourages customers to connect with you on other platforms.

- Newsletter Sign Up: Include a newsletter sign up form to capture email addresses and build your email marketing list.

- Additional Resources: Consider adding links to blog posts, guides, or other valuable content that can help customers make informed decisions.

5. Mobile-Friendly Navigation:

With the increasing use of mobile devices for online shopping, it's crucial to ensure your navigation is mobile-friendly. Here are some tips:

- Responsive Design: Choose a responsive theme that adapts to different screen sizes. Test your navigation on various devices to ensure it works seamlessly.

- Mobile Menu: Use a mobile-friendly menu, often referred to as a "hamburger" menu, which collapses the main navigation into a compact, accessible icon. This menu expands when clicked, making it easy for mobile users to navigate your store.

- Touch-Friendly Elements: Ensure that all navigation elements are touch-friendly. This means having adequately

sized buttons and links that are easy to tap without accidentally hitting adjacent items.

- *Streamlined Content:* On mobile devices, space is limited, so prioritize the most important content and navigation options. Avoid clutter and ensure a smooth scrolling experience.

Final Touches for a Polished Store Design

Now that you've chosen a theme, customized it, and ensured your navigation is user-friendly, it's time to add the final touches to your store design. These elements can enhance the overall aesthetic and functionality of your store, making it more appealing to customers.

1. High-Quality Images:

High-quality product photos are vital for promoting your products effectively. Blurry or low-resolution images can deter customers and undermine your brand's professionalism. Here are some pointers for using images effectively:

- *Consistent Style:* Use a consistent style for all your product images. This includes lighting, background, and image dimensions. Consistency creates a unified and professional appearance.

- *Multiple Angles:* Provide multiple images for each product, showing different angles and details. This helps customers get a better sense of the product and reduces uncertainty.

- **_Zoom Function:_** Implement a zoom function that allows customers to see close-up details of your products. This feature can enhance the shopping experience, especially for products with intricate details.

2. Engaging Copy:

The text on your store, including product descriptions, about pages, and blog posts, plays a crucial role in engaging customers and conveying your brand's personality. Here are some tips for crafting intriguing copy:

- **_Clear and Concise:_** Ensure your copy is clear, concise, and easy to read. Avoid using jargon and complicated terminology that might confuse customers.

- **_Brand Voice:_** Develop a consistent brand voice that reflects your brand's personality. Whether it's playful, professional, or inspirational, your voice should resonate with your target audience.

- **_SEO Optimization:_** Optimize your copy for search engines by incorporating relevant keywords. This can help improve your store's visibility in search results and attract more organic traffic.

3. Trust Signals:

Building trust with your customers is vital for driving sales and sustaining loyalty. Incorporate trust signals throughout your store to reassure customers and enhance their confidence in your brand:

- *Customer Reviews:* Display customer reviews and testimonials prominently on your product pages. Positive reviews can influence purchasing decisions and build credibility.

- *Security Badges:* Include security badges and trust seals to indicate that your store is secure and that customer data is protected. This can be particularly reassuring for first-time visitors.

- *Clear Policies:* Make your shipping, return, and privacy policies easily accessible. Clearly explain your policies to set expectations and address any concerns customers might have.

4. Call-to-Action Buttons:

Call-to-action (CTA) buttons guide customers towards desired actions, such as adding products to the cart, signing up for a newsletter, or completing a purchase. Effective CTAs are crucial for driving conversions. Here are some tips for optimizing your CTAs:

- *Clear and Compelling:* Use clear and compelling language for your CTA buttons. Instead of generic terms like "Click Here," use action-oriented phrases like "Buy Now," "Sign Up," or "Learn More."

- *Visible and Contrasting:* Ensure your CTA buttons stand out by using contrasting colors that draw attention. They should be easily visible and clickable on both desktop and mobile devices.

- Strategic Placement: Place your CTAs strategically throughout your store, especially on high-traffic pages like the homepage, product pages, and checkout page. Make it easy for your customers to proceed to the next step.

5. Consistent Branding:

Consistency is key to creating a professional and memorable brand. Ensure that all elements of your store design, from the logo and color scheme to fonts and imagery, align with your brand identity. Consistent branding helps build recognition and trust over time.

6. Testing and Iteration:

Once you've implemented your store design, it's important to test and iterate to ensure everything works seamlessly and meets your customers' needs. Here's how to approach this process:

- User Testing: Conduct user testing to gather feedback on your store's design and usability. Ask friends, family, or even potential customers to navigate your store and provide their insights.

- A/B Testing: Use A/B testing to compare different design elements and determine what works best. Test variations of CTA buttons, product page layouts, and other key elements to optimize your store's performance.

- **_Analytics and Metrics:_** Monitor your store's analytics to track key metrics such as bounce rate, conversion rate, and average session duration. Use this information to search for areas for improvement and make data-driven decisions.

7. Continuous Improvement:

The world of e-commerce is dynamic, and customer preferences can change over time. Stay updated with the latest design trends and continually seek ways to improve your store. Regularly refresh your content, update your images, and introduce new features to keep your store engaging and relevant.

Designing your Shopify store is an exciting and creative process that sets the foundation for your e-commerce success. By choosing the right theme, customizing it to reflect your brand, and creating a user-friendly navigation system, you're well on your way to building a compelling online store.

Remember, the key to a successful store design is understanding your customers' needs and preferences. By prioritizing user experience, maintaining consistent branding, and continually testing and improving your design, you can create a store that not only looks great but also drives sales and builds lasting customer relationships.

As you get started on this journey, don't be afraid to experiment and let your creativity shine. Your Shopify store is a reflection of your unique vision and passion, and with the right design, you can create an online shopping experience that delights and inspires your customers.

CHAPTER THREE
Sourcing Products for Your Store

In this chapter, we'll get into the specifics of sourcing products for your store. This is the exciting part of the journey since the products you choose will form your store's identity and, eventually, its success. We will go over how to identify dependable suppliers, the criteria for choosing them, the best dropshipping suppliers and marketplaces, and how to properly vet and engage with suppliers. Let's get started.

Finding Reliable Suppliers

Finding reliable suppliers is like finding a gold mine in the dropshipping world. Your suppliers are the backbone of your business, and choosing the right ones can make or break your store. But how do you find these elusive, reliable suppliers?

1. Conduct Research Online: The internet is a wealth of knowledge. Use search engines, supplier directories, and dropshipping forums to find potential suppliers. Websites like Alibaba, AliExpress, and Oberlo are excellent starting points. These platforms have a vast array of suppliers, each offering different products and services.

2. Supplier Directories: Supplier directories are databases of suppliers categorized by industry, product, or location. Some popular directories include SaleHoo, Worldwide Brands, and Doba. These directories often vet suppliers, providing a layer of security and reliability.

3. *Networking and Trade Shows:* Attend industry trade shows and networking events. These are fantastic opportunities to meet suppliers face-to-face, see their products, and build relationships. Websites like Trade Show News Network can help you find relevant events.

4. *Social Media and Forums:* Join dropshipping groups on social media platforms like Facebook and Reddit. Engage with the community by asking for recommendations and sharing your own experiences. Often, other dropshippers can point you toward reliable suppliers they've worked with.

5. *Contact Manufacturers Directly:* Sometimes, the best way to find a reliable supplier is to go straight to the source. Contact manufacturers of the products you're interested in and ask if they offer dropshipping services or can recommend a distributor who does.

Criteria for Choosing Suppliers

Not all suppliers are created equal. Once you have a list of potential suppliers, you need to vet them carefully. Here are some essential qualities to be mindful of:

1. *Product Quality:* The quality of the products you sell will directly impact your store's reputation. Request samples from your potential suppliers to evaluate the product quality. Look for durable materials, good craftsmanship, and accurate product descriptions.

2. Reliability and Reputation: Research your suppliers' reputation. Look for reviews and ratings on platforms like Trustpilot, Google Reviews, or within supplier directories. A reliable supplier should have positive feedback and a track record of timely deliveries.

3. Communication: Good communication is crucial. Your supplier should be responsive, clear, and easy to reach. Test their communication by asking questions and noting how quickly and thoroughly they respond.

4. Pricing and Minimum Order Quantities (MOQs): Compare pricing among different suppliers to ensure you're getting a competitive rate. Also, check if they have MOQs. Some suppliers require you to order a certain amount of product, which can be a barrier for new dropshippers.

5. Shipping Times and Costs: Shipping can make or break a customer's experience. Ensure your supplier offers reasonable shipping times and costs. Ideally, they should provide tracking information and handle international shipping if necessary.

6. Return and Refund Policies: Understand the supplier's return and refund policies. These policies should be fair and clear, both for you and your customers. A supplier with a strict or vague return policy might lead to unhappy customers.

7. Technology and Integration: Your supplier should offer technology solutions that integrate seamlessly with your Shopify store. This includes inventory management, automated order processing, and real-time product updates.

Top Dropshipping Suppliers and Marketplaces

Now that you know what to look for in a supplier, let's explore some of the top dropshipping suppliers and marketplaces you can consider for your store.

1. AliExpress: AliExpress is one of the most popular dropshipping platforms. It provides a wide selection of products at cheap pricing. Many suppliers on AliExpress are experienced with dropshipping, making it easier to set up your store. The downside is longer shipping times, especially if your customers are in the U.S. or Europe.

2. Oberlo: Oberlo is a marketplace that works with Shopify, making it simple to import products directly into your store. It primarily sources products from AliExpress but offers a curated selection of suppliers to ensure better quality and reliability.

3. SaleHoo: SaleHoo is a supplier directory that vets suppliers, ensuring they are reliable and offer quality products. It includes suppliers from various industries and offers tools to help you find profitable niches and trending products.

4. Doba: Doba aggregates products from various suppliers, simplifying the process of finding and managing suppliers. It offers a wide range of products and features like product data integration, making it easier to manage your inventory.

5. Wholesale Central: This platform features a database of wholesale suppliers in the United States.

It offers a range of products and is free to use. However, it's essential to vet each supplier individually as the platform doesn't guarantee supplier reliability.

6. *Printful:* If you're interested in selling custom-printed products like apparel, accessories, and home decor, Printful is a great option. It integrates seamlessly with Shopify and offers high-quality printing and fast shipping times.

7. *Spocket:* Spocket focuses on suppliers from the U.S. and Europe, offering faster shipping times compared to suppliers based in Asia. It integrates with Shopify and offers a range of products, from apparel to electronics.

8. *Modalyst:* Modalyst provides a curated list of suppliers offering high-quality products, including name-brand items. It integrates with Shopify and automates many aspects of dropshipping, making it easier to manage your store.

How to Vet and Communicate with Suppliers

Once you've identified potential suppliers, it's time to vet them and establish strong communication channels. Here's a step-by-step guide to help you navigate the process:

1. *Initial Contact:* Reach out to your potential suppliers via email or phone. Introduce yourself and your business or brand and express your interest in their products. Ask about their dropshipping services, shipping times, return policies, and any other relevant information.

2. Ask for Samples: Request product samples to evaluate quality. This step is crucial to ensure that the products meet your standards and match their descriptions.

3. Check References and Reviews: Look for reviews from other dropshippers or businesses that have worked with the supplier. Ask the supplier for references if possible. Contact these references to obtain personal reports of their experiences.

4. Assess Communication: Throughout your interactions, pay close attention to how the supplier communicates. Are their responses immediate and clear? Do they answer all your questions satisfactorily? Good communication is essential for a smooth business relationship.

5. Negotiate Terms: Don't be afraid to negotiate terms with your suppliers. Discuss pricing, shipping costs, MOQs, and payment terms. A good supplier should be willing to work with you to find mutually beneficial terms.

6. Request Documentation: Ask for any necessary documentation, such as business licenses, certifications, or insurance. This can help verify the legitimacy of the supplier.

7. Test the Supplier: Place a small order to test the supplier's process. Monitor how long it takes for the order to be processed, shipped, and delivered. Evaluate the packaging and condition of the products upon arrival.

8. Build a Relationship: Once you've chosen your supplier, continue to build a strong relationship. Regular communication, timely payments, and mutual respect go a long way in ensuring a successful partnership.

9. Use Contracts: Consider using contracts to formalize your agreements. A contract can outline terms and conditions, expectations, and any other relevant details. This can provide protection for both parties and help prevent misunderstandings.

Sourcing products for your Shopify store is a critical step in building a successful dropshipping business. By finding reliable suppliers, carefully vetting them, and maintaining strong communication, you can ensure that your store offers high-quality products and excellent customer service. Remember, your suppliers are your partners in this journey, and choosing the right ones can set you on the path to success.

Adding Products to Your Store

Adding products to your Shopify store is one of the most exciting parts of setting up your business. This is where your store starts to take shape and gain its unique identity. But it's not just about uploading images and setting prices. To make your store stand out, you need to approach this task with a strategic mindset.

1. Identify Your Niche: Before you start adding products, it's crucial to identify your niche. What kind of products do you intend to sell? Who is your target audience? Having a clear understanding of your niche helps you select products that resonate with your potential customers.

2. Create Product Categories: Organize your products into categories. This not only makes it easier for you to manage your inventory but also helps your customers navigate your store. For example, if you're selling home decor, you might have categories like "Wall Art," "Furniture," "Lighting," and "Accessories."

3. Choose High-Quality Images: Visual appeal is everything in online shopping. Use high-quality images for your products. Ideally, your images should be clear, well-lit, and show the product from multiple angles. If possible, attach pictures of the product in use.

4. Set Competitive Prices: Pricing can make or break a sale. Investigate your competition to determine the market prices for your products. Aim for a balance between competitive pricing and maintaining healthy profit margins. Remember to factor in costs like shipping, transaction fees, and marketing.

5. Optimize for SEO: Search Engine Optimization (SEO) is vital for driving organic traffic to your store. Incorporate relevant and appropriate keywords into your product titles, descriptions, and tags. This helps search engines understand what your products are and makes it easier for potential customers to find you.

6. Write Compelling Product Descriptions: Your product descriptions should be informative and persuasive. Highlight each product's advantages, benefits, and distinguishing selling points.

7. Set Up Inventory Management: Keep track of your inventory to avoid overselling or stockouts. Shopify offers built-in inventory management tools that allow you to monitor stock levels, set up alerts for low inventory, and manage product variants.

8. Enable Customer Reviews: Customer reviews can significantly influence purchasing decisions. Enable reviews on your product pages to build trust and provide social proof. Encourage your customers to leave reviews by following up after purchase and offering incentives like discounts on future orders.

Importing Products from Suppliers

Once you've laid the groundwork for adding products to your store, it's time to import them from your suppliers. This process involves selecting the right products, ensuring they are listed correctly, and maintaining a seamless flow of inventory from your suppliers to your store.

1. Choose Your Suppliers: As discussed in previous chapters, finding reliable suppliers is crucial. Whether you're using platforms like AliExpress, Oberlo, or Spocket, ensure that your suppliers offer high-quality products, reliable shipping, and good customer service.

2. Use Shopify Apps: Shopify offers several apps that make importing products a breeze. Apps like Oberlo, Spocket, and Dropified allow you to browse supplier catalogs, select products, and import them directly into your store with just a few clicks.

3. Import Product Information: When importing products, ensure that all necessary information is included. This typically includes product titles, descriptions, prices, images, and variants (like size and color). Most Shopify apps allow you to customize this information before importing.

4. Review and Edit: Don't rely solely on the supplier's product information. Review and edit the product details to align with your brand's voice and style. Ensure that the product descriptions are engaging, the images are high-quality, and the pricing is competitive.

5. Automate Inventory Syncing: To avoid overselling, set up inventory syncing with your suppliers. Many dropshipping apps offer real-time inventory updates, ensuring that your stock levels are always accurate. This helps prevent stockouts and keeps your customers happy.

6. Monitor Product Performance: After importing your products, keep an eye on their performance. Use Shopify's analytics tools to track sales, customer behavior, and inventory levels. This data helps you identify popular products, optimize your pricing, and make informed decisions about your inventory.

7. Stay Updated with Supplier Changes: Suppliers may update their product offerings, prices, or shipping policies. Stay informed about these changes to ensure that your store remains up-to-date. Regularly check supplier notifications and update your product listings accordingly.

Writing Effective Product Descriptions

Product descriptions are your primary tool for convincing potential customers to make a purchase. A well-crafted description not only informs but also persuades and inspires confidence in your products. Here's how to write effective product descriptions that sell.

1. Know Your Audience: The first step in writing compelling product descriptions is understanding your audience. Who are your customers? What are their needs, preferences, and pain points? Customize your descriptions to appeal to your target audience.

2. Highlight Benefits, Not Just Features: While it's essential to list the features of your product, focusing on the benefits can make a stronger impact. Explain how the product addresses and fixes an issue or improves the life of the customer. For example, instead of saying "This water bottle is 32 oz," say "Stay hydrated all day with this large 32 oz water bottle, perfect for workouts and busy days."

3. Tell a Story: Storytelling can make your product more relatable and appealing. Describe a scenario where the product is used or tell a story about its creation. For example, "Imagine sipping your morning coffee from this handcrafted mug, made by skilled artisans using traditional techniques."

4. Use Sensory Language: Engage your customers' senses by using descriptive language. Words like "soft," "crisp," "vibrant," and "luxurious" can help customers visualize and feel the product. For example, "Wrap yourself in the soft, luxurious comfort of our 100% cotton bathrobe."

5. Be Clear and Concise: While it's important to be descriptive, avoid long-winded paragraphs. Keep your descriptions precise, straightforward, and easy to read. Use bullet points to highlight key features and benefits, and break up the text with subheadings if necessary.

6. Include Specifications: Provide detailed specifications to help customers make informed decisions. This can include dimensions, materials, weight, and care instructions. For example, "Dimensions/Sizes: 12 x 8 x 6 inches. Material: 100% organic cotton. Machine washable."

7. Incorporate Keywords: Remember to include relevant keywords in your product descriptions for SEO purposes. This helps your products rank higher in search engine results and makes it easier for customers to find your store. Use keywords naturally and refrain from keyword stuffing.

8. Add a Call to Action: Encourage customers to take the next step with a clear call to action. Phrases like "Add to Cart," "Shop Now," and "Don't Miss Out" are all phrases that can motivate customers to make a purchase. Make sure your call to action is prominent and persuasive.

9. Use Social Proof: Incorporate customer reviews, ratings, and testimonials in your product descriptions. Social proof can build trust and provide reassurance to potential customers. For example, "Join thousands of satisfied customers who love our eco-friendly water bottles!"

10. A/B Testing: Finally, don't be afraid to experiment with different descriptions. Conduct A/B testing to see which descriptions perform best. Use the data to refine your approach and continually improve your product listings.

Setting Competitive Pricing

Pricing your products competitively is a combination of art and science. The right pricing strategy can attract customers, boost sales, and ensure profitability. Here's a comprehensive guide to help you set competitive prices for your Shopify store:

Understand Your Costs: Before setting your prices, you need to understand all the costs involved in running your dropshipping business. This includes the cost of goods sold (COGS), shipping fees, transaction fees, marketing expenses, and other overhead costs. Knowing your total costs ensures that you set prices that cover your expenses and generate a profit.

Research Competitors: Conduct market research to understand how your competitors are pricing their products. Look at both direct competitors (those selling the same products) and indirect competitors (those selling similar products). Analyzing competitor pricing helps you position your products in the market and identify opportunities to differentiate your store.

Determine Your Pricing Strategy: There are several pricing strategies you can use, depending on your business goals and market conditions.

Here are some common strategies:

Cost-Plus Pricing: This involves adding a fixed percentage or amount to the cost of your products to determine the selling price. For example, if your COGS is $20 and you want a 50% markup, you would price the product at $30.

Competitive Pricing: This strategy involves setting your prices based on your competitors' prices. You can choose to price your products lower, higher, or the same as your competitors, depending on your value proposition.

Value-Based Pricing: This method involves setting prices based on their perceived value of your products to customers. If you offer high-quality, unique, or branded products, you can charge a premium price.

Psychological Pricing: This strategy uses pricing tactics that appeal to customers' emotions and perceptions. For example, pricing a product at $29.99 instead of $30.00 makes it appear cheaper, even though the difference is minimal.

Consider Your Target Audience: Your pricing should align with the expectations and purchasing power of your target audience. If you're targeting budget-conscious customers, competitive or cost-plus pricing might be more effective. If you're targeting premium customers, value-based pricing might be a better fit.

Factor in Shipping Costs: Shipping costs can significantly impact your pricing strategy. Decide whether you'll offer free shipping, flat-rate shipping, or charge shipping based on the order value or weight. If you offer free shipping, make sure to factor the shipping costs into your product prices to avoid eroding your profit margins

Use Discounts and Promotions Wisely: Discounts and promotions can boost sales and attract new customers, but they should be used strategically. Offering too many discounts can devalue your products and hurt your profitability. Consider running limited-time promotions, bundling products, or offering discounts to repeat customers to encourage loyalty.

Monitor and Adjust Prices: Pricing is not a one-time task. Regularly review and adjust your prices based on market conditions, competitor actions, and customer feedback. Use analytics tools to track the performance of your products and identify trends that may require pricing adjustments.

Communicate Value: Regardless of your pricing strategy, it's essential to communicate the value of your products effectively. Highlight the features, benefits, and unique selling points in your product descriptions and marketing materials. Customers should understand why your products are worth the price you're asking.

Test Different Prices: Don't be afraid to experiment with different price points to find the optimal pricing for your products. Use A/B testing to compare the performance of different prices and gather data on customer behavior. Testing helps you make data-driven decisions and optimize your pricing strategy.

Consider Currency Conversion: If you're selling internationally, consider how currency conversion affects your pricing. Use Shopify's built-in currency converter or third-party apps to display prices in your customers' local currency. This improves the shopping experience and reduces obstructions to purchase.

Adding products to your Shopify store and setting competitive pricing are crucial steps in building a successful dropshipping business. By thoughtfully curating your product offerings and pricing them strategically, you can attract and retain customers, drive sales, and ensure profitability. Remember, the key to success lies in understanding your niche, researching your competitors, and continuously optimizing your strategies. Keep your store fresh and engaging by regularly updating your products and refining your pricing approach. With these strategies in place, you are well on your way to creating a thriving dropshipping store on Shopify.

CHAPTER FOUR
Managing Your Store

This chapter will focus on three crucial aspects: order fulfillment and inventory management, automating order fulfillment, tracking inventory levels, and handling returns and refunds. Managing these elements effectively is key to running a smooth and successful dropshipping business.

Order Fulfillment and Inventory Management

Understanding Order Fulfillment

When a customer places an order on your Shopify store, the process of getting the product from the supplier to your customer begins. This is known as order fulfillment. In a traditional retail model, you'd handle this yourself, but in dropshipping, this responsibility falls largely on your suppliers. Your role is to ensure that this process runs smoothly.

Order fulfillment involves several steps:

1. Order Confirmation: Once an order is placed, you need to confirm it with your supplier.

2. Processing the Order: The supplier then processes the order, prepares the product, and ships it to your customer.

3. Tracking and Delivery: Keeping track of the order until it is delivered to your customer. Even though you are not directly handling the products, it's crucial to monitor this process to ensure timely delivery and customer satisfaction.

Inventory Management

In traditional retail, inventory management is a major task involving storage, handling, and stocktaking. In dropshipping, while you don't hold inventory yourself, managing inventory levels is still important. You need to ensure that your suppliers have the products you list on your store in stock and ready to ship.

Why Inventory Management Matters:

1. Avoiding Stockouts: Running out of stock can lead to missed sales opportunities and disappointed customers.

2. Reducing Overselling: Overselling happens when you sell more products than your supplier has in stock, leading to delays and unhappy customers.

3. Maintaining Customer Trust: Consistently having products available builds trust with your customers.

To manage inventory effectively, establish strong communication lines with your suppliers and use tools and apps that integrate with Shopify to track inventory levels in real-time.

Automating Order Fulfillment

Manual order fulfillment can be time-consuming and prone to errors. Automation streamlines this process, saving you time and reducing the risk of mistakes. Shopify offers several apps and tools that can automate order fulfillment, making it almost hands-free.

Choosing the Right Automation Tools

When selecting automation tools, consider the following:

1. Integration with Shopify: Ensure the tool integrates seamlessly with your Shopify store.

2. Supplier Integration: The tool should work well with your suppliers' systems.

3. Features and Flexibility: Look for features like bulk order processing, automatic tracking updates, and customizable workflows.

Popular Automation Tools for Shopify

1. Oberlo: A popular tool for automating order fulfillment. It allows you to import products directly into your Shopify store, and when an order is placed, Oberlo automatically fulfills it with your supplier.

2. Dropified: Another powerful automation tool that offers features like automated order fulfillment, tracking updates, and product import.

3. Spocket: Ideal for finding high-quality products from suppliers in the US and Europe, with automated fulfillment features.

Setting Up Automation

Setting up automation in your Shopify store involves:

1. Installing the App: Choose and install the automation app that best fits your needs from the Shopify App Store.

2. Configuring Settings: Customize the app settings to match your workflow. For example, you can set it to automatically fulfill orders as soon as they are placed.

3. Testing: Before going live, run a few test orders to ensure everything works smoothly.

Automation can significantly reduce your workload, allowing you to focus on other important aspects of your business, such as marketing and customer service.

Tracking Inventory Levels

Real-time inventory tracking ensures that your store always reflects the actual stock levels of your suppliers. This helps in avoiding the dreaded "out of stock" scenario and keeps your customers happy.

Tools for Inventory Tracking

Several tools can help you keep track of inventory levels:

1. Shopify's Built-In Tools: Shopify offers basic inventory tracking features that allow you to track the quantity of each product variant and receive notifications when stock is low.

2. Inventory Management Apps: Apps like Stock Sync, Katana, and TradeGecko offer more advanced inventory management features, such as real-time stock updates and multi-supplier integration.

Best Practices for Inventory Management

1. Regular Communication with Suppliers: Maintain regular communication with your suppliers to stay updated on stock levels and potential delays.

2. Using Multiple Suppliers: Relying on a single supplier can be risky. Diversify your supplier base to ensure you always have alternative sources for your products.

3. Setting Up Low Stock Alerts: Configure your inventory management tools to send alerts when stock levels drop below a certain threshold.

By keeping a close eye on inventory levels, you can avoid stockouts and ensure a smooth shopping experience for your customers.

Handling Returns and Refunds

Returns and refunds are an unavoidable part of every retail business. How you handle them can significantly impact customer satisfaction and your store's reputation. A clear and fair returns policy builds trust and encourages customers to shop with confidence.

Creating a Returns Policy

A well-defined returns policy should include:

1. Timeframe for Returns: Specify the time period within which customers can return products (e.g., 30 days from purchase).

2. Condition of Returned Items: Clearly state the condition in which items must be returned (e.g., unused, in original packaging).

3. Return Shipping Costs: Indicate who will bear the cost of return shipping (e.g., customer or store).

4. Refund Process: Explain how and when refunds will be processed.

Communicating Your Returns Policy

Make your returns policy easily accessible on your website. Place it in prominent locations such as the footer, FAQ section, and checkout page. Ensure the language is clear and straightforward.

Handling Returns Efficiently:

1. Automate Return Requests: Use apps like Returnly, AfterShip Returns Center, or Loop Returns to automate and streamline the return request process.

2. Provide Return Labels: Offering prepaid return labels can simplify the process for customers and improve their experience.

3. Track Returns: Keep track of returned items and their status to ensure timely processing and refunds.

Processing Refunds:

Refunds should be processed promptly to maintain customer trust. Once a return is received and inspected, process the refund using the same payment method the customer used for the purchase. Inform the customer when the refund has been processed and provide an estimated timeline for when they can expect the funds to be credited.

Managing Refund Disputes:

Occasionally, you might encounter disputes over refunds. Handle these situations carefully and professionally:

1. Listen to the Customer: Understand their concerns and try to find a mutually acceptable solution.

2. Be Transparent: Clearly explain your returns policy and the reasons for any decisions made.

3. Offer Alternatives: If a refund isn't possible, consider offering store credit or an exchange as an alternative.

By managing returns and refunds effectively, you can turn a potentially negative experience into a positive one, building long-term loyalty with your customers.

Final Thoughts

Managing your Shopify store involves a lot more than just listing products and waiting for sales to roll in. Effective order fulfillment, inventory management, automation, and handling returns and refunds are critical components that can make or break your dropshipping business.

By automating as much of the process as possible, you can save time and reduce the risk of errors. Real-time inventory tracking helps you avoid stockouts and maintain customer satisfaction. And by handling returns and refunds efficiently and fairly, you can build a loyal customer base that trusts and values your brand.

As you continue to grow and refine your store, always keep your customers' experience at the forefront of your mind. Happy customers are the key to a successful dropshipping business.

Customer Service Essentials

In the competitive world of e-commerce, excellent customer service can set your store apart from the rest. It's not just about selling products; it's about creating a positive shopping experience that encourages customers to return and recommend your store to others. Here are some reasons why customer service is important:

1. Customer Retention: Keeping existing customers is often more cost-effective than acquiring new ones. Excellent customer service helps in retaining customers.

2. Reputation: Positive customer experiences lead to positive reviews and word-of-mouth recommendations, which can boost your store's reputation.

3. Trust and Loyalty: Providing reliable customer service builds trust and fosters customer loyalty, which is crucial for long-term success.

Key Elements of Customer Service

1. Responsiveness: Responding quickly to customer inquiries and issues is critical. Customers appreciate timely responses and resolutions.

2. Empathy: Understanding and empathizing with your customers' needs and concerns shows that you care about their experience.

3. Consistency: Consistent service quality ensures that customers know what to expect every time they interact with your store.

4. Knowledge: Being knowledgeable about your products and policies helps you provide accurate and helpful information to customers.

Providing Excellent Customer Support

To provide excellent customer support, you need to be accessible through various channels. Here are some often used customer support channels:

1. Email Support: An essential channel for handling detailed inquiries and issues. Make sure your email support is prompt and informative.

2. Live Chat: Offers real-time support to customers while they are browsing your store. Apps like Tidio or Zendesk Chat can be integrated with Shopify.

3. Phone Support: Although less common in dropshipping, phone support can provide a personal touch for more complex issues.

4. Social Media: Many customers prefer to reach out via social media platforms like Facebook, Instagram, or Twitter. Ensure you monitor these channels regularly.

Developing a Customer Support Strategy

Having a strategy in place ensures that your customer support is consistent and effective. Here's how to develop one:

1. Define Response Times: Set clear response time goals for each support channel. For example, respond to emails within 24 hours and live chat within minutes.

2. Create a Knowledge Base: Develop a comprehensive FAQ section on your website to help customers find answers to common questions quickly.

3. Train Your Team: If you have a team, ensure they are well-trained in your products, policies, and customer service best practices.

4. Use Support Tools: Utilize tools like Help Scout, Zendesk, or Freshdesk to manage customer inquiries and track resolutions.

Personalizing Customer Interactions

Personalization can enhance the customer experience significantly. Here's how to add a personal touch:

1. Use Customer Names: Address customers by their names in communications.

2. Tailor Responses: Customize your responses based on the customer's inquiry history and preferences.

3. Follow-Up: After resolving an issue, follow up to ensure the customer is satisfied with the resolution.

Handling Customer Inquiries and Complaints

Effective communication is key to handling customer inquiries and complaints. Here are some tips:

1. Listen Actively: Pay attention to what the customer is saying without interrupting. This shows respect and helps you understand their issue fully.

2. Be Clear and Concise: Provide clear, concise, and honest answers. Avoid jargon and make your explanations straightforward.

3. Stay Professional: Maintain a professional tone, even if the customer is upset. This helps de-escalate the situation.

Resolving Inquiries

When a customer reaches out with a question or concern, your goal is to resolve it efficiently and satisfactorily. Here's a step-by-step approach:

1. Acknowledge the Inquiry: Let the customer know that you have received their inquiry and are looking into it.

2. Gather Information: Ask relevant questions to gather all necessary information to understand and resolve the issue.

3. Provide a Solution: Offer a clear and actionable solution. If the issue cannot be resolved immediately, explain the steps you will take and provide a timeline.

4. Confirm Resolution: Once the issue is resolved, confirm with the customer that they are satisfied with the outcome.

Handling Complaints

Handling complaints effectively can turn a negative experience into a positive one. Here's how:

1. *Acknowledge the Complaint:* Show empathy and acknowledge the customer's feelings. A simple "I understand how frustrating this must be for you" can go a long way.

2. *Apologize Sincerely:* Offer a genuine apology for any trouble caused.

3. *Find a Solution:* Work with the customer to find a satisfactory resolution. This might involve offering a refund, replacement, or discount.

4. *Follow Up:* After resolving the complaint, follow up to ensure the customer is happy with the resolution and to show that you value their business.

Common Customer Inquiries and How to Respond

1. *Product Information:* Customers often have questions about product details. Ensure you have thorough knowledge of your products and provide clear, accurate information.

2. *Order Status:* Provide customers with real-time updates on their order status. Using apps that send automatic updates can help.

3. *Shipping Issues:* Address any shipping delays or issues promptly. Work with your supplier to resolve the issue and keep the customer informed.

4. Returns and Refunds: Clearly communicate your returns and refunds policy and ensure the process is straightforward and fair.

Building Long-term Customer Relationships

Building long-term relationships with your customers is essential for sustained success. Loyal customers are more likely to make repeat purchases, refer your store to others, and leave positive reviews. Here's how to cultivate these relationships:

Providing Exceptional Customer Experiences:

Creating memorable and positive experiences can turn one-time buyers into loyal customers. Here are some strategies:

1. Exceed Expectations: Go above and beyond what the customer expects. This could be as simple as a handwritten thank-you note or a small freebie with their order.

2. Consistent Quality: Ensure that the quality of your products and services is consistently high.

3. Personal Touch: Personalize interactions and make customers feel valued and appreciated.

Building Trust and Credibility:

Trust is the foundation of any long-term relationship. Here's how to build it:

1. Be Transparent: Be honest and transparent about your products, policies, and any issues that arise.

2. Deliver on Promises: Always deliver what you promise, whether it's product quality, delivery times, or customer support.

3. Showcase Reviews and Testimonials: Positive reviews and testimonials can build credibility and trust with potential customers.

Engaging with Customers:

Regular engagement with your customers keeps your store top of mind and fosters a sense of community. Here's how to engage effectively:

1. Social Media: Use social media platforms to interact with your customers, share updates, and showcase new products.

2. Email Marketing: Send regular newsletters with updates, promotions, and personalized recommendations.

3. Customer Feedback: Encourage and act on customer feedback to show that you value their opinions and are committed to improving.

Loyalty Programs:

Loyalty programs reward your repeat customers and encourage them to keep coming back. Here's how to set up an effective loyalty program:

1. Points System: Implement a points-based system where customers earn points for purchases, reviews, or referrals, which can be redeemed for discounts or free products.

2. Tiered Rewards: Create different tiers of rewards based on customer spending levels. Higher tiers can offer exclusive discounts, early access to new products, or special gifts.

3. Special Offers: Provide exclusive offers and discounts to loyalty program members.

Handling Long-term Relationships

Maintaining long-term relationships requires ongoing effort. Here are some tips:

1. Stay in Touch: Regularly check in with your customers through email or social media to maintain the relationship.

2. Celebrate Milestones: Recognize and celebrate customer milestones, such as anniversaries of their first purchase or their birthdays, with special offers or messages.

3. Continuous Improvement: Continuously seek feedback and make improvements to your products and services based on customer input.

Final Thoughts

Managing your Shopify store effectively involves more than just listing products and processing orders. Providing excellent customer service, handling inquiries and complaints efficiently, and building long-term relationships with your customers are crucial components of a successful dropshipping business.

By focusing on these aspects, you can create a positive shopping experience that encourages repeat business and fosters customer loyalty. Remember, happy customers are the key to a thriving dropshipping store. So, invest in your customer service, be responsive and empathetic, and always strive to exceed your customers' expectations.

CHAPTER FIVE
Marketing Your Dropshipping Store

Driving Traffic to Your Store

Now comes the crucial part – getting people to visit your store.

Any internet business relies on traffic to succeed. Without visitors, even the best-designed store with the most amazing products will struggle to make sales. In this chapter, we'll explore various strategies to drive traffic to your store.

Introduction to Digital Marketing

Digital marketing is your ticket to reaching a global audience. Any internet business relies on traffic to operate. Unlike traditional marketing, which focuses on physical media such as newspapers and television advertisements, digital marketing makes use of online channels.

This allows you to target specific audiences, track performance, and adjust your strategies in real-time. Digital marketing includes a variety of channels, such as social media, search engines, email marketing, and more. Let's break these down.

Utilizing Social Media for Marketing

Social media platforms are bustling hubs where millions of people spend a significant portion of their day. By leveraging social media, you can reach a vast audience and engage with potential customers directly. Here's how you can effectively use social media for marketing your dropshipping store:

Choosing the Right Platforms:

Not all social media platforms are created equal. Each has a distinct user base and types of content that do well. Here's a short look at some of the most popular platforms:

- *Facebook:* With over 2.8 billion monthly active users, Facebook is a versatile platform. It's great for running ads, sharing updates, and building a community through groups.

- *Instagram:* Perfect for visually appealing products. Instagram is excellent for sharing high-quality images and short videos. Its shopping feature also allows users to buy directly from posts.

- *Twitter:* Ideal for real-time updates and engaging in conversations. Twitter can be useful for building brand personality and handling customer service.

- *Pinterest:* Great for niche products, especially in categories like fashion, home decor, and DIY. Pinterest users often search for inspiration and ideas, making it a good platform for product discovery.

- *TikTok:* Popular among younger audiences, TikTok is excellent for short, engaging video content. It's a powerful platform for viral marketing.

Creating Engaging Content:

Content is king on social media. Your posts should be engaging, informative, and tailored to your audience's interests. Here are some content ideas:

- **Product Showcases:** Highlight your products with high-quality images and videos. Show them in use to help potential customers envision how they can benefit from them.

- **Behind-the-Scenes:** Share a glimpse of the process behind your business. This could include how products are sourced, packaged, or stories about your team.

- **Customer Testimonials:** Share feedbacks and testimonials from satisfied customers. User-generated content can build trust and authenticity.

- **Educational Posts:** Create content that educates your audience about your products or industry. This could be in the form of how-to guides, ideas, or industry news.

- **Interactive Content:** Engage your audience with polls, quizzes, and Q&A sessions. Interactive content can boost engagement and build a sense of community.

Running Social Media Ads:

Algorithm modifications may restrict your social media reach organically.

To reach a broader audience, consider running paid ads. Most platforms offer robust advertising tools with detailed targeting options. Here's a quick overview:

- Facebook Ads: You can target users based on demographics, interests, behavior, and even lookalike audiences. Facebook Ads Manager allows you to create various ad formats, including image ads, video ads, carousel ads, and more.

- Instagram Ads: Managed through Facebook Ads Manager, Instagram ads can be highly effective. To grab attention, use eye-catching visuals and persuasive copy.

- Twitter Ads: Promoted tweets can help you reach a larger audience. Twitter ads are great for promoting timely offers and engaging in conversations.

- Pinterest Ads: Promoted pins blend seamlessly with organic content. They're ideal for visually appealing products and can drive traffic directly to your store.

- TikTok Ads: TikTok's ad platform allows you to create engaging video ads. Given TikTok's algorithm, even small businesses can go viral with the right content.

Search Engine Optimization (SEO)

SEO is the practice of optimizing your online store to rank higher in search engine results pages (SERPs). Higher rankings mean more visibility and, ultimately, more traffic. Here's how you can optimize your Shopify store for SEO:

Keyword Research:

Keywords are the terms and phrases users enter into search engines. Identifying the right keywords is the foundation of your SEO strategy. Here's how to do it:

- **Brainstorm:** Think about what words and phrases your target audience might use to find your products. Consider the specific terms that describe your products, their benefits, and uses.

- **Use Tools:** Tools like Google Keyword Planner, Ahrefs, and SEMrush can help you find relevant keywords and gauge their search volume and competition.

- **Competitor Analysis:** Analyze your competition by looking up the keywords they are ranking for.

Tools like Ahrefs and SEMrush can provide insights into your competitors' top-performing keywords.

On-Page SEO:

On-page SEO refers to optimizing individual pages on your website to rank higher in search engines.

Here are a few essential points to remember:

- **Title Tags:** Your main keyword should appear in an unique, descriptive title tag on every page. To ensure that it displays appropriately in search results, keep it to fewer than 60 characters.

- **Meta Descriptions:** Meta descriptions are brief summaries that appear below your title tag in search results. They should be compelling and include your primary keyword. Aim for 150-160 characters.

- **Headers:** To organize your content, use header tags (H1, H2, H3). Your primary keyword should appear in the H1 tag, which is typically the page's title.

- **URL structure:** Make sure your URLs are descriptive and brief. Include your primary keyword and avoid unnecessary numbers and characters.

- **Alt Text for Images:** Search engines can't "see" images, so use alt text to describe them. Include relevant keywords where appropriate.

Content Marketing:

Creating high-quality, relevant content can boost your SEO efforts. Here's how to approach content marketing for your Shopify store:

- **Blogging:** Start a blog on your Shopify store and regularly publish posts related to your products and industry. Blog posts can target long-tail keywords, answer common questions, and provide value to your audience.

- **Product Descriptions:** Write detailed, unique product descriptions for each item in your store. Avoid using manufacturer descriptions because duplicate information can harm your SEO.

- Guides and Tutorials: Create comprehensive guides and tutorials that relate to your products. These can attract backlinks and establish your store as an authority in your niche.

Technical SEO:

Technical SEO entails optimizing your website's infrastructure so that search engines may easily crawl and index it. Here are some critical areas to concentrate on:

- Site Speed: A fast-loading site improves user experience and can boost your rankings. Use tools such as Google PageSpeed Insights to discover and resolve speed issues.

- Mobile-Friendliness: Google uses mobile-first indexing, so make sure your site is mobile-friendly. Shopify themes are generally responsive, but it's essential to test your site on various devices.

-Sitemap: Generate and submit a sitemap to the search engines. Shopify automatically generates a sitemap for your store, which you can submit via Google Search Console.

-SSL Certificate: Use an SSL certificate to safeguard your website. HTTPS is a ranking factor, and it assures visitors that their data is safe.

Driving Traffic with Email Marketing

Email marketing is still one of the most effective strategies to drive traffic and purchases.

By building an email list, you can reach out to potential and existing customers directly. Here's how to create and execute a successful email marketing strategy:

Building Your Email List:

- Opt-In Forms: Place opt-in forms strategically on your website, such as on the homepage, product pages, and blog posts. Offer an incentive, like a discount or free resource, to encourage sign-ups.

-Pop-ups: Use exit-intent pop-ups to capture users who are about to exit your website. These can offer a discount or remind them to sign up for your newsletter.

- Lead Magnets: Provide valuable content, like eBooks, guides, or exclusive access, in exchange for email addresses.

Crafting Engaging Emails:

- Welcome Series: Set up a series of welcome emails in order to introduce new subscribers to your brand. Share your story, highlight popular products, and offer a discount to encourage their first purchase.

- Newsletters: To keep your audience engaged, send out newsletters on a regular basis.

Include updates, new product announcements, and exclusive offers.

- *Promotional Emails:* Run targeted email campaigns for sales, holidays, or special events. Create a sense of urgency with limited-time offers and clear calls to action.

Segmenting Your Audience:

Segmentation allows you to send more personalized and relevant emails. Divide your email list into segments based on factors like purchase history, behavior, and demographics. For example:

- *New Customers:* Send a series of onboarding emails with tips on how to use their purchased products.

- *Loyal Customers:* Reward repeat customers with exclusive discounts and early access to new products.

- *Inactive Customers:* Win back inactive customers with re-engagement campaigns offering special incentives.

Analyzing and Optimizing

Regularly analyze your email campaign performance to understand what's working and what isn't. Key metrics to track include:

- *Open Rates:* Open Rate: The percentage of recipients who read your email. Crafting engaging subject lines can increase open rates significantly.

- *Click-Through Rates (CTR):* The percentage of recipients who click on links in your email. Increase CTR by ensuring your emails are visually appealing, and contain clear, compelling calls to action.

- **Conversion Rates:** The percentage of recipients who perform the desired action, such as purchasing. Improve conversion rates by ensuring your landing pages are optimized and relevant to the email content.

- **Bounce Rate:** This is the percentage of emails that were unable to be sent. Maintain a clean email list by frequently eliminating invalid addresses.

Effective Advertising Strategies

Google Ads:

Google Ads allows you to display your ads on Google's search results and across its network of partner sites. Here's how to get started:

- **Keyword Research:** Use Google's Keyword Planner to identify relevant keywords for your products. Concentrate on keywords with high search volume and minimal competition.

- **Creating Ads:** Write compelling ad copy that highlights the benefits of your products. Include a strong call to action.

- **Targeting:** Use precise targeting options to reach your ideal customers. You can target based on demographics, location, and interests.

*- **Retargeting:*** Set up retargeting campaigns to reach users who have visited your site but didn't make a purchase. Retargeting ads can remind them of your products and encourage them to return.

Facebook and Instagram Ads:

Facebook and Instagram's ad platforms offer robust targeting options and a variety of ad formats. Here's how to make the most of them:

*- **Audience Targeting:*** Analyze your target audience by demographics, interests, and behaviors. Use lookalike audiences to reach new potential customers who resemble your existing ones.

*- **Ad Formats:*** Experiment with various ad forms, such as picture advertisements, video ads, carousels, and collection ads. Test which formats are most effective with your target audience.

*- **Creative Content:*** Create visually appealing and engaging ad creatives. High-quality photos and videos can grab attention and generate clicks.

*- **A/B Testing:*** Conduct A/B testing to evaluate various ad variations. Test different headlines, images, and calls to action to identify what works best.

Pinterest Ads:

Pinterest Ads can be particularly effective for niche products. Here's how to get started:

- Promoted Pins: Create promoted pins that blend seamlessly with organic content. Ensure your pins are visually appealing and include a clear call to action.

- Targeting: Use Pinterest's targeting options to reach users based on interests, demographics, and search keywords.

- Visual Appeal: Focus on high-quality visuals that showcase your products. Pinterest is a visual platform, so attractive images are essential.

- Tracking Performance: Monitor your ad performance using Pinterest's analytics tools. Track metrics like clicks, saves, and conversions to optimize your campaigns.

Partnering with Affiliate Marketers:

Affiliate marketing involves partnering with individuals or other businesses who promote your products in exchange for a commission on sales. Here's how to build a successful affiliate program:

Setting Up an Affiliate Program

- Choose a Platform: Use affiliate marketing platforms like ShareASale, CJ Affiliate, or Shopify's own affiliate apps to manage your program.

- **Commission Structure:** Determine a competitive commission rate that incentivizes affiliates to promote your products. Common rates range from 5% to 20% per sale.

- **Affiliate Resources:** Provide your affiliates with resources like banners, product images, and promotional copy. This makes it easier for them to market your products efficiently.

- **Tracking and Payment:** Ensure you have a reliable system for tracking affiliate sales and paying commissions. Most affiliate platforms handle this for you.

Recruiting Affiliates:

- **Existing Customers:** Reach out to your existing customers and offer them a chance to join your affiliate program. Satisfied customers can be enthusiastic promoters.

- **Bloggers and Influencers:** Identify bloggers and influencers in your niche and invite them to join your program. Their established audiences can drive significant traffic to your store.

- **Affiliate Networks:** Join an affiliate network to connect with potential affiliates. These networks can help you find affiliates who are already experienced in promoting similar products.

Managing and Optimizing:

- Communication: Maintain regular communication with your affiliates. Provide them with updates, new product information, and promotional opportunities.

- Performance Analysis: Track the performance of your affiliates and identify top performers. Focus on nurturing these relationships and providing additional support.

- Incentives: Offer bonuses and incentives for high-performing affiliates. This can motivate them to promote your products even more aggressively.

Building a Community

Building a community around your brand can drive traffic and foster loyalty. Here's how to build and develop a community:

Engaging with Your Audience:

- Social Media: Use social media to engage with your audience regularly. Reply to comments, ask questions, and encourage user-generated content.

- User-Generated Content: Request images and product reviews from your consumers. Feature their content on your social media and website.

- Online Forums and Groups: Join and participate in online forums and groups related to your niche. Engage prospective customers in conversation and provide insightful information.

Hosting Events:

-Webinars and Live Streaming: Use webinars and live streams to interact with your audience in real time. Share valuable information, respond to questions, and promote your products.

- Contests and Giveaways: Run contests and giveaways to generate excitement and engagement. Encourage participants to share your content in order to boost visibility.

Utilizing Content Marketing:

Content marketing entails creating and sharing useful information in order to attract and engage your target audience. Here's how you use content marketing successfully:

Blogging:

- Regular Posts: Publish regular blog posts related to your products and industry. Aim for at least one post per week to keep your content fresh and relevant.

- SEO Optimization: Optimize your blog posts for SEO by including relevant keywords, internal links, and engaging meta descriptions.

- Guest Posts: Invite industry experts to contribute guest posts to your blog. This can bring new perspectives and attract their followers to your site.

Video Marketing:

- Product Videos: Create high-quality videos showcasing your products. Highlight their features, benefits, and use cases.

- Tutorials and How-Tos: Produce tutorial videos that show customers how to use your products. These can be particularly effective for complex or unique items.

- Behind-the-Scenes: Share behind-the-scenes videos to give your audience a glimpse into your business. This can humanize your brand and build trust.

Google Ads and Shopping Campaigns

Google Ads offers another powerful platform to drive traffic to your dropshipping store. With Google Ads, you can target users who are actively searching for products like yours, making it a highly effective advertising method.

Understanding Google Ads

Google Ads uses a pay-per-click (PPC) approach, which means you pay every time someone clicks on your ad.

Here are the main types of Google Ads you can use:

- Search Ads: Text ads that appear at the top of Google search results when users search for specific keywords.

- Display Ads: Display adverts are image or video adverts that show on websites in Google's Display Network.

- **Shopping Ads:** Product-based ads that appear at the top of Google search results with images, prices, and product details.

- **Video Ads:** Ads that appear on YouTube and other video partner sites.

Setting Up Your Google Ads Campaign

To get started with Google Ads, follow these steps:

1. Create a Google Ads Account: Sign up for a Google Ads account and set up your billing information.

2. Install Google Ads Conversion Tracking: Add a piece of code to your Shopify store to track conversions and measure the success of your ads.

3. Keyword Research: Use tools like Google Keyword Planner to find relevant keywords for your products. Concentrate on keywords with high search volume and minimal competition.

Creating Effective Search Ads

Search ads are text-based and appear when users search for specific keywords. Here's how to create effective search ads:

- **Headline:** Write a compelling headline that includes your primary keyword and grabs attention.

- **Description:** Provide a brief description of your product and include a call-to-action.

- *URL:* Ensure the URL is relevant to the ad and takes users to a specific landing page.

- *Ad Extensions:* Use ad extensions to include additional information like site links, call buttons, and reviews.

Setting Up Shopping Campaigns

Shopping ads are particularly effective for dropshipping stores as they showcase your products directly in search results. Here's how to set up shopping campaigns:

1. Create a Merchant Center Account: Sign up for Google Merchant Center and link it to your Google Ads account.

2. Upload Product Feed: Create and upload a product feed containing detailed information about your products, including titles, descriptions, prices, and images.

3. Create Shopping Campaign: In Google Ads, create a new shopping campaign and select the products you want to advertise.

4. Optimize Product Listings: Ensure your product titles and descriptions are optimized with relevant keywords to improve visibility.

Budgeting and Bidding

Like Facebook and Instagram ads, setting a budget and choosing the right bidding strategy is crucial for your Google Ads campaigns:

- *Daily Budget:* Set a daily budget for your campaigns to control your spending.

- *Bidding Strategy:* Choose a bidding strategy that aligns with your campaign goals, such as target cost-per-action (tCPA), target return on ad spend (tROAS), or maximize clicks.

Analyzing and Optimizing

Regularly monitor your Google Ads performance and make adjustments to improve results:

- *Impressions and Clicks:* Track the number of times your ads were displayed and clicked.

- *Conversion Rate:* Measure the percentage of clicks that resulted in a purchase or other desired action.

- *Quality Score:* Google assigns a quality score to each keyword based on the relevance of your ads and landing pages. A higher quality score might result in reduced costs and better ad placement.

- *Cost Per Click (CPC):* Monitor your average CPC to ensure you're not overspending on clicks.

Influencer Marketing

Influencer marketing entails collaborating with people who have a significant and engaged following on social media. By utilizing their influence, you can reach a larger audience and gain the trust of potential consumers.

Finding the Right Influencers

Choosing the right influencers is critical to the success of your influencer marketing campaigns. Here's how to find the right influencers:

- **Relevance:** Look for influencers who create content related to your niche. Their audience should be interested in your products.

- **Engagement:** Analyze the engagement rates of potential influencers. High engagement means the audience is active and responsive.

- **Authenticity:** Choose influencers who share your brand's values and can honestly promote your products.

Types of Influencer Collaborations

There are several ways to collaborate with influencers to promote your dropshipping store:

- **Product Reviews:** Send influencers your products for them to review and share their honest opinions with their followers.

- Sponsored Posts: Pay influencers to create and share content featuring your products. Ensure the content aligns with their style and resonates with their audience.

- Giveaways: Partner with influencers to run giveaways. This can create enthusiasm and raise your brand's awareness.

- Affiliate Marketing: Set up an affiliate program where influencers earn a commission for every sale they drive to your store. This gives them an incentive to actively market your products.

Building Relationships with Influencers

Building strong relationships with influencers can lead to more successful and long-term partnerships:

- Personalized Outreach: When reaching out to influencers, personalize your message and explain why you think they'd be a great fit for your brand.

- Provide Value: Offer influencers something of value, such as free products, exclusive discounts, or monetary compensation.

- Communication: Maintain open and regular communication with your influencers. Keep them informed about new product launches, promotions, and any relevant updates. This helps them feel more connected to your brand and can enhance their promotional efforts.

Measuring the Success of Influencer Campaigns

It is important to track the performance of your influencer marketing campaigns to understand their impact and optimize future collaborations. Here's how to measure success:

- *Engagement Metrics:* Monitor likes, comments, shares, and other forms of engagement on the influencer's posts. A high level of interaction shows that the content was well received by its target audience.

- *Traffic and Sales:* Use tracking links or discount codes to measure the traffic and sales generated from the influencer's promotion. This helps you attribute results directly to their efforts.

- *Return on Investment (ROI):* Calculate the ROI by comparing the revenue generated from the campaign to the cost of the collaboration. A positive ROI is indicative of a successful campaign.

- *Brand Awareness:* Track changes in your social media following, website traffic, and overall brand visibility. Increased brand awareness is a key benefit of influencer marketing.

Combining Strategies for Maximum Impact

While each advertising strategy has its strengths, combining multiple strategies can create a more comprehensive and effective marketing plan. Here's how to integrate Facebook and

Instagram Ads, Google Ads, and Influencer Marketing for maximum impact:

Coordinated Campaigns

Run coordinated campaigns across different platforms to create a cohesive brand message and maximize reach. For example:

- ***Pre-Launch Hype:*** Use influencer marketing to build anticipation before a product launch. Influencers can tease the new product and generate buzz among their followers.

- ***Launch Day Push:*** On launch day, run targeted Facebook, Instagram, and Google Ads to drive traffic and sales. Use the momentum created by influencers to boost ad performance.

- ***Retargeting:*** Use retargeting ads on Facebook, Instagram, and Google to reach users who visited your site but didn't make a purchase. This keeps your brand top of mind and encourages conversions.

Consistent Branding

Ensure your branding is consistent across all platforms and campaigns. This involves using the exact same logo, color scheme, and tone of voice. Consistent branding helps create a cohesive and recognizable brand identity.

Cross-Promotion

Cross-promote your marketing efforts to maximize their impact. For example:

- *Social Media Shoutouts:* When an influencer posts about your product, share their content on your own social media channels. This increases visibility and reinforces the message.

- *Email Marketing:* Include information about your social media ads and influencer collaborations in your email newsletters. This can result in additional traffic and engagement.

- *Blog and Content Marketing:* Write blog posts or create videos that highlight your influencer collaborations and ad campaigns. This provides additional content for your audience and enhances your overall marketing strategy.

Final Thoughts on Marketing Your Dropshipping Store

Marketing your dropshipping store effectively requires a multifaceted approach. By leveraging the power of Facebook and Instagram Ads, Google Ads and Shopping Campaigns, and Influencer Marketing, you can drive traffic, increase sales, and build a strong brand presence.

Remember, marketing is a continuous process that requires continuous testing, analysis, and optimization. Stay up-to-date with the latest trends and best practices, and don't be afraid to try new strategies to see what works best for your store.

Action Steps:

1. Set up Your Facebook and Instagram Ads: Create a Facebook Business Page, set up Facebook Ads Manager, and install Facebook Pixel on your Shopify store.

2. Define Your Target Audience: Use Facebook's detailed targeting options to create custom and lookalike audiences.

3. Create Engaging Ad Content: Design high-quality visuals and write compelling ad copy. Experiment with different ad formats.

4. Launch Your Google Ads Campaigns: Create a Google Ads account, conduct keyword research, and set up search and shopping campaigns.

5. Find and Collaborate with Influencers: Identify relevant influencers, build relationships, and create mutually beneficial collaborations.

6. Measure and Optimize: Regularly analyze the performance of your ad campaigns and influencer partnerships. Make data-driven adjustments to improve results.

By following these steps and leveraging the strategies outlined, you will be well on your way to successfully marketing your dropshipping store and driving sustainable growth.

CHAPTER SIX
Analyzing and Improving Store Performance

Optimizing your dropshipping store begins with understanding how it's currently performing. You can't fix what you don't know is broken, right? Let's go right into the process of analyzing and improving your store's performance.

Assessing Current Performance

First things first, you need to take a snapshot of where your store stands right now. Look at your sales, traffic, and customer engagement over the past few months. This gives you a baseline to measure improvement against.

1. Sales Data: Analyze your sales data to see which products are selling well and which aren't. Look at your revenue, profit margins, and sales volume. Identify trends and patterns. Are there certain times of the year when sales spike? Do some products sell better in specific seasons?

2. Customer Data: Understanding your customers is crucial. Who are they? Where do they come from? What are their purchasing habits? Use the data from your Shopify store to create customer profiles. This will help you tailor your marketing efforts more effectively.

3. Website Traffic: Examine your website traffic to understand where your visitors are coming from. Do they find you via search engines, social media, or personal visits? Look at the bounce rate (the percentage of visitors who leave after viewing only one page) and the average time spent on your site. These metrics give you an idea of how engaging your site is.

4. Conversion Rates: This is the percentage of visitors who make a purchase. A low conversion rate indicates that while you're getting traffic, you're not convincing visitors to buy. Analyzing this can help you identify areas for improvement, such as your product descriptions, pricing, or checkout process.

Identifying Areas for Improvement

Once you've assessed your current performance, the next step is to identify areas for improvement. Here are some common areas where dropshipping stores often need a bit of tweaking:

1. Website Design and Usability: Is your website easy to navigate? Does it look professional? A poorly designed website can drive away potential clients. Consider using a clean, modern design that makes it easy for visitors to find what they're looking for.

2. Product Pages: Your product pages need to be informative and compelling. Ensure you have high-quality images, detailed descriptions, and clear pricing. Highlight the benefits of your products and include customer reviews if possible.

3. Checkout Process: A complicated or lengthy checkout process can lead to cart abandonment. Simplify your checkout process by minimizing the number of steps and ensuring it works smoothly on both desktop and mobile devices.

4. Loading Speed: Slow-loading websites can frustrate visitors and lead to higher bounce rates. Optimize your site's loading speed by compressing images, using efficient coding practices, and choosing a reliable hosting provider.

5. Customer Service: Offering exceptional customer service can distinguish you from competition. Make it easy for customers to contact you with questions or issues. Consider adding a live chat feature to your site for real-time support.

Key Metrics to Track

Now that we've covered how to analyze and identify areas for improvement, let's talk about the key metrics you should be tracking. These metrics will help you gauge the health of your store and guide your optimization efforts.

1. Traffic: Monitor the number of visitors to your store. Look at both the total number of visitors and the unique visitors (those who visit your store for the first time). This helps you understand how well your marketing efforts are driving traffic to your store.

2. Conversion Rate: As mentioned earlier, your conversion rate is the percentage of visitors who make a purchase. A healthy conversion rate for eCommerce stores is typically between 1% and 2%. If your rate is lower, it may indicate issues with your product pages or checkout process.

3. Average Order Value (AOV): This is the average amount spent by customers per order. To figure this out, divide your total revenue by the number of orders. A higher AOV means you're getting more value from each customer. You can increase AOV by offering upsells, cross-sells, or bundle deals.

4. Customer Acquisition Cost (CAC): This is the amount you spend to acquire a new customer. To calculate it, divide your total marketing expenses by the number of new customers acquired during a specific period. Lowering your CAC means you're spending less to gain each new customer, improving your profitability.

5. Customer Lifetime Value (CLTV): This metric estimates the total revenue a customer will generate over their lifetime with your store. It's crucial for understanding the long-term value of your customers and guiding your marketing and retention strategies.

6. Bounce Rate: This is the percentage of visitors who exit your website after merely viewing only one page. A high bounce rate can indicate that your site isn't engaging or relevant to visitors. Aim to maintain your bounce rate under 40%.

7. Cart Abandonment Rate: This is the percentage of customers who add items to their cart but don't complete the purchase. A high cart abandonment rate can indicate issues with your service: Excellent customer service can set your store apart from the competition. Make sure you have a clear and accessible way for customers to contact you with questions or concerns. Answer questions and respond to concerns in a timely and professional manner.

8. Marketing Strategies: Assess your current marketing strategies. Are you using the right channels to reach your target audience? Experiment with different marketing tactics, such as email campaigns, social media advertising, and influencer partnerships, to see what works best for your store.

Sales Metrics To Track:

1. Revenue: This is the total amount of money your store is bringing in. Tracking your revenue over time helps you understand overall growth and seasonal trends.

2. Average Order Value (AOV): This metric tells you the average amount a customer spends per transaction. Increasing your AOV can greatly increase your revenue. Strategies to increase AOV include upselling, cross-selling, and offering discounts on bundled products.

3. Gross Profit: Gross profit is your revenue minus the cost of goods sold (COGS). It gives you a clearer picture of your profitability. Aim to increase your gross profit by negotiating better rates with suppliers or optimizing your pricing strategy.

4. Net Profit: This is your gross profit minus all other expenses, such as marketing, shipping, and operating costs. Net profit gives you a true sense of your store's financial health.

Customer Metrics To Track:

1. Customer Acquisition Cost (CAC): CAC is the amount of money you spend to acquire a new customer. This includes marketing and advertising expenses. Lowering your CAC can help increase your profitability.

2. Customer Lifetime Value (CLV): CLV refers to the total amount of money a customer is predicted to spend in your store over their lifetime. Increasing CLV can significantly boost your revenue. Strategies to increase CLV include loyalty programs, personalized marketing, and excellent customer service.

3. Customer Retention Rate: This metric measures the percentage of customers who make repeat purchases. A high retention rate implies that customers are satisfied and loyal. Focus on building strong relationships with your customers to improve retention.

Website Metrics To Track:

1. Traffic Sources: Understanding where your traffic comes from (e.g., organic search, paid ads, social media) helps you allocate your marketing budget more effectively.

2. Bounce Rate: A high bounce rate indicates that visitors are leaving your site without engaging. Analyze the pages with high bounce rates and make improvements to keep visitors on your site longer.

3. Conversion Rate: This is the percentage of visitors who do the intended action, such as placing a purchase. Improving your conversion rate can significantly boost your sales. Test different elements on your site, such as headlines, images, and calls to action, to see what works best.

4. Cart Abandonment Rate: This is the percentage of customers who add items to their cart but don't complete the purchase. High cart abandonment rates can be reduced by simplifying the checkout process, offering multiple payment options, and sending follow-up emails to remind customers of their abandoned carts.

Using Google Analytics and Shopify Analytics

To effectively track these metrics, you need the right tools. Google Analytics and Shopify Analytics are two powerful tools that can provide you with detailed insights into your store's performance.

Setting Up Google Analytics

Google Analytics is a free tool that provides a wealth of information about your website traffic and user behavior. Here's how to set it up:

1. Create an Account: Go to the Google Analytics website and create a new account. Follow the prompts to set up your account and property (your Shopify store).

2. Get Tracking ID: Once your account is set up, you'll receive a tracking ID. This is a unique code that you'll need to add to your Shopify store to start tracking data.

3. Add Tracking ID to Shopify: In your Shopify admin, go to Online Store > Preferences. Scroll down to the Google Analytics section and paste your tracking ID. Click Save.

4. Enable Enhanced Ecommerce: To get more detailed data about your ecommerce performance, enable Enhanced Ecommerce in Google Analytics. In your Shopify admin, go to Settings > Checkout and ensure the Enhanced Ecommerce Tracking box is checked.

Understanding Google Analytics Reports

Once Google Analytics is set up, you can access a variety of reports to analyze your store's performance. Here is how to understand your google analytics report:

1. Audience Report: This report provides information about your visitors, including demographics, interests, and location. Understanding your audience helps you tailor your marketing efforts more effectively.

2. Acquisition Report: This report shows where your traffic is coming from, such as search engines, social media, or direct visits. Use this information to determine which marketing channels are the most effective.

3. Behavior Report: This report provides insights into how visitors interact with your site. You can see which pages are most popular, how long visitors stay on your site, and where they drop off.

4. Conversion Report: This report shows how well your site is converting visitors into customers. You can track sales, revenue, and other goals you've set up in Google Analytics.

Using Shopify Analytics

Shopify also provides a range of analytics tools to help you track and analyze your store's performance:

1. Dashboard: The Shopify dashboard provides an overview of your store's key metrics, such as total sales, online store sessions, and top products. Use this dashboard to get a quick snapshot of your store's performance.

2. Sales Reports: Shopify's sales reports provide detailed information about your sales, including revenue, order volume, and average order value. Use these reports to identify trends and patterns in your sales data.

3. Customer Reports: These reports provide insights into your customer base, including customer acquisition, retention, and lifetime value. Use this information to customize your marketing and customer service activities.

4. Behavior Reports: These reports show how visitors interact with your site, including page views, bounce rate, and conversion rate. Use this information to identify areas for improvement in your site's design and usability.

5. Marketing Reports: These reports show the effectiveness of your marketing campaigns, including traffic sources, conversion rates, and return on investment (ROI). Use this information to optimize your marketing strategies.

Making Data-Driven Decisions

With all this data at your fingertips, the next step is to use it to make informed decisions that will help you optimize your store for success. Here's how:

Setting Goals:

Before you can make data-driven decisions, you need to set clear, measurable goals for your store. These goals should be specific, attainable, and in line with your overall business objectives. For example, you might set a goal to increase your monthly sales by 20% or reduce your cart abandonment rate by 10%.

Analyzing Data:

Once you've set your goals, use the data from Google Analytics and Shopify Analytics to track your progress. Look for trends and patterns to assist you figure out what is and isn't working.

For example, if you notice that your conversion rate is lower than expected, analyze the behavior reports to see where visitors are dropping off.

Testing and Experimenting:

One of the key benefits of having detailed data is the ability to test different strategies and see what works best. Here are some areas where you can experiment:

1. Website Design: Test different layouts, colors, and fonts to see what appeals most to your audience. Use A/B testing to compare different versions of your site and determine which one performs better.

2. Product Pages: Experiment with different product descriptions, images, and pricing strategies. See which combinations lead to higher conversion rates and sales.

3. Checkout Process: Simplify your checkout process and test different payment options. See if offering multiple payment methods or a guest checkout option reduces cart abandonment.

4. Marketing Strategies: Try different marketing tactics, such as email campaigns, social media ads, and influencer partnerships. Use the data from your marketing reports to see which strategies generate the most traffic and conversions.

Making Adjustments:

Based on your analysis and experiments, make adjustments to your store to optimize performance. This might involve redesigning your website, updating product pages, streamlining your checkout process, or shifting your marketing focus. The key is to continuously monitor your data and make data-driven decisions to improve your store's performance.

Continuous Improvement:

Optimizing your store is not a one-time task. It is a continuing process that necessitates regular monitoring and improvement. Regularly review your key metrics, analyze your data, and make adjustments as needed. Stay up-to-date with industry trends and best practices to ensure your store remains competitive and successful.

Optimizing your Shopify dropshipping store for success involves a combination of analyzing performance, tracking key metrics, using powerful analytics tools, and making data-driven decisions. By setting clear goals, regularly monitoring your data, experimenting with different strategies, and making continuous improvements, you can ensure your store is always on the path to growth and success.

Remember, the journey to optimization is ongoing. Stay committed to analyzing your performance, learning from your data, and making informed decisions. With dedication and the right strategies, your Shopify dropshipping store will thrive in the competitive ecommerce landscape.

Scaling Your Dropshipping Business

Scaling your dropshipping business involves increasing your capacity to handle more orders, improving your processes, and expanding your reach. It's about taking your business from a small operation to a larger, more profitable enterprise.

Evaluating Your Current Capacity:

Before you can scale, you need to understand your current capacity. Assess your current operations, including your supplier relationships, inventory management, order fulfillment, and customer service. Identify any bottlenecks or limitations that could hinder your ability to grow.

1. Supplier Reliability: Ensure that your suppliers can handle increased order volumes without compromising on quality or delivery times. Establish solid ties with multiple suppliers to reduce risks.

2. Inventory Management: Use inventory management tools to keep track of stock levels and prevent overselling. This is especially important as you scale and your order volumes increase.

3. Order Fulfillment: Streamline your order fulfillment process to ensure timely delivery. Consider partnering with fulfillment centers or third-party logistics providers to handle increased order volumes efficiently.

4. Customer Service: As your business grows, you'll need to maintain high levels of customer service. Invest in customer service tools and train your team to handle more inquiries and issues effectively.

Financial Readiness:

Scaling requires investment. Evaluate your financial situation to ensure you have the necessary funds to support growth. This includes investing in marketing, inventory, technology, and human resources. Consider options like reinvesting profits, seeking investors, or obtaining business loans to finance your scaling efforts.

Expanding Your Product Line:

One of the most effective ways to scale your dropshipping business is by expanding your product line. Offering a wider range of products can attract more customers, increase sales, and boost your overall revenue.

Identifying Opportunities:

Start by analyzing your current product performance. Identify your best-selling products and look for related items that your customers might also be interested in. Use market research tools and customer feedback to identify gaps in your product offerings.

1. Customer Feedback: Pay attention to customer reviews and feedback. Are there products they wish you offered? Use this information to guide your product expansion strategy.

2. Market Trends: Stay informed about industry trends and emerging products. Use tools like Google Trends, industry reports, and competitor analysis to identify popular and trending products.

3. Supplier Catalogs: Explore the catalogs of your current suppliers for new products. Building on existing supplier relationships can make it easier to expand your product line.

Testing New Products:

Before fully committing to new products, test them to ensure there's demand. Add a few new items to your store and monitor their performance. Use data from your Shopify and Google Analytics to track sales, customer interest, and feedback.

1. *Product Listings:* Create compelling product listings with high-quality images, detailed descriptions, and competitive pricing. Highlight the advantages and distinguishing features of each product.

2. *Marketing:* Promote your new products through email campaigns, social media, and other marketing channels. Use targeted ads to reach potential customers who are likely to be interested in the new products.

3. *Customer Feedback:* Encourage customers to leave reviews and feedback on your new products. Use this information to make any necessary adjustments and improve your product offerings.

Outsourcing and Automating Tasks

As your business grows, managing everything on your own can become overwhelming. Outsourcing and automating tasks can help you save time, reduce stress, and focus on strategic growth activities.

Identifying Tasks to Outsource:

Start by identifying tasks that are time-consuming, repetitive, or outside your area of expertise. Common tasks to outsource include:

1. Customer Service: Hiring virtual assistants or customer service agencies can help you manage customer inquiries, returns, and complaints more efficiently.

2. Order Fulfillment: Partnering with third-party logistics providers (3PLs) can streamline your order fulfillment process, allowing you to handle more orders without additional stress.

3. Marketing: Hiring a marketing agency or freelance experts can help you create and execute effective marketing campaigns. This involves managing social media, email marketing, and paid advertising.

4. Content Creation: Outsource content creation tasks like blog posts, product descriptions, and graphic design to freelancers or content agencies. This ensures you have high-quality content without spending too much time on it.

Automating Processes:

Automation tools can help you streamline various aspects of your business, from inventory management to marketing.

Here are some significant areas for automation:

1. Inventory Management: Use inventory management software to automatically track stock levels, reorder products, and prevent overselling. Tools like Oberlo, Stock Sync, and TradeGecko can integrate with your Shopify store.

2. Order Processing: Automate order processing tasks like order confirmation emails, tracking updates, and shipping notifications. Tools like ShipStation and ShipBob can help automate these processes.

3. Marketing Automation: Use marketing automation tools to schedule social media posts, send personalized email campaigns, and track marketing performance. Tools like Mailchimp, Klaviyo, and Hootsuite can help you automate your marketing efforts.

4. Customer Relationship Management (CRM): Implement a CRM system to manage customer interactions, track sales leads, and automate follow-up emails. Tools like HubSpot, Salesforce, and Zoho CRM can integrate with your Shopify store.

Strategies for Growing Your Customer Base

Expanding your customer base is crucial for scaling your dropshipping business. By attracting new customers and retaining existing ones, you can increase sales and drive sustainable growth.

Enhancing Your Marketing Efforts:

1. Content Marketing: Create valuable and engaging content that attracts and educates your target audience. This comprises blog articles, videos, infographics, and social media content. Use SEO best practices to optimize your content for search engines and drive organic traffic to your store.

2. Email Marketing: Build an email list and use email marketing campaigns to nurture relationships with your customers. Send out personalized emails containing product recommendations, special offers, and relevant material. Use solutions like Mailchimp or Klaviyo to automate your email marketing campaigns.

3. Social Media Marketing: Leverage social media platforms to connect with your audience and promote your products. Create a consistent posting schedule, engage with your followers, and use paid ads to reach a larger audience. Platforms like Facebook, Instagram, and Pinterest are particularly effective for ecommerce businesses.

4. Paid Advertising: Invest in paid advertising to reach a larger audience and drive targeted traffic to your store. Use platforms like Google Ads, Facebook Ads, and Instagram Ads to create targeted ad campaigns. To maximise ROI, monitor your ad performance and adjust your strategies accordingly.

Building Customer Loyalty:

1. Personalized Marketing: Use customer information to create personalized marketing strategies. Send personalized product recommendations, birthday offers, and special discounts to make customers feel valued and appreciated.

2. Excellent Customer Service: Provide exceptional customer service to build trust and loyalty. Respond promptly to customer inquiries, resolve issues quickly, and go the extra mile to ensure customer satisfaction.

3. Engage with Customers: Build a community around your brand by engaging with customers on social media, responding to comments and messages, and encouraging user-generated content. This helps create a loyal customer base that feels connected to your brand.

Expanding Your Reach:

1. International Expansion: Consider expanding your business to international markets. This can open up new opportunities and increase your customer base. Research the demand for your products in different countries and adjust your marketing strategies to cater to international audiences.

2. Affiliate Marketing: Implement an affiliate marketing program to encourage others to promote your products. Affiliates earn a commission for every sale they generate, providing an incentive to drive traffic and sales to your store. Use tools like Refersion or ShareASale to manage your affiliate program.

3. Collaborations and Partnerships: Partner with other businesses in your niche to cross-promote products and reach new audiences. Collaborations can include joint marketing campaigns, co-branded products, or exclusive discounts for each other's customers.

Scaling your dropshipping business requires a strategic approach that includes expanding your product line, outsourcing and automating tasks, and implementing effective strategies to grow your customer base. When you continuously analyze your performance, invest in the right tools and resources, and focus on customer satisfaction, you can successfully take your dropshipping business to new heights.

Growth doesn't happen overnight. It requires commitment, perseverance, and an eagerness to adapt and learn. Keep refining your strategies, experimenting with new ideas, and staying up-to-date with industry trends. With the right approach, your Shopify dropshipping store will thrive and become a profitable and sustainable business.

CHAPTER SEVEN
Legal and Financial Requirements

When you start a dropshipping business, it's tempting to focus only on the exciting parts—finding products, creating your website, and making sales. However, understanding and complying with legal requirements is just as crucial. Not only can it save you from potential fines and lawsuits, but it also builds trust with your customers and suppliers.

Business Licenses and Permits

First, let's talk about business licenses and permits. Depending on where you live and where you plan to sell your products, you might need a business license. This license essentially gives you the legal right to operate your business. The specific requirements vary by country, state, and even city, so it's essential to check with your local government to determine what you need.

E-commerce Regulations

Next, we have e-commerce regulations. Because you're running an online business, you need to be aware of the rules that govern online transactions. These can include data protection laws, consumer rights, and electronic transaction regulations.

For instance, in the European Union, the General Data Protection Regulation (GDPR) has strict rules about how you can collect, store, and use customer data.

International Trade Laws

If you plan to sell products internationally, you also need to consider international trade laws. Different countries have various regulations about what can be imported and exported, customs duties, and taxes. It's crucial to understand these laws to avoid any legal complications and ensure smooth delivery of your products to customers worldwide.

Intellectual Property Rights

Finally, let's talk about intellectual property rights. This is particularly important if you plan to sell branded products. You need to ensure that you're not infringing on any trademarks or copyrights. Selling counterfeit products can lead to severe penalties, including hefty fines and legal action from the brand owners. Always verify that your suppliers are authorized to sell the products and that you're not violating any intellectual property laws.

Setting Up a Business Entity

Now that we have a basic understanding of the legal landscape, let's dive into setting up your business entity. Choosing the right business structure is a critical decision that can affect your taxes, personal liability, and overall business operations.

Sole Proprietorship:

A sole proprietorship is the most easy and most common structure for a small business. It's simple to set up, and you have full control over your business. However, the downside is that there's no legal separation between you and your business. This means that if your business incurs debts or legal issues, your personal assets could be at risk.

Partnership:

If you're starting your dropshipping business with a partner, you might consider a partnership. In this structure, you and your partner share the profits, losses, and responsibilities of the business. Like a sole proprietorship, a partnership is relatively easy to establish, but it also means that both partners are personally liable for the business's debts and legal issues.

Limited Liability Company (LLC):

An LLC is a popular choice for small businesses, including dropshipping businesses, because it offers the benefits of both a corporation and a partnership. With an LLC, your personal assets are protected from business debts and legal actions, and you can enjoy the flexibility of pass-through taxation, where the business's profits and losses pass through to your personal tax return.

Corporation:

A corporation is a more complex business structure that provides the strongest protection for its owners from personal liability. However, it comes with more regulations, higher costs, and double taxation—once on the corporation's profits and again on the shareholders' dividends. This structure is usually more suitable for larger businesses with significant growth potential.

Registering Your Business:

Once you've decided on the structure, the next step is to register your business. This process involves choosing a business name, filing the necessary paperwork with your local government, and obtaining any required licenses and permits. You may also need to get an Employer Identification Number (EIN) from the IRS if you're in the United States. This number is being used for tax purposes and is required when opening a business bank account and hiring personnel.

Tax Obligations for Dropshipping

Navigating tax obligations can be one of the more daunting aspects of running a dropshipping business, but it's essential to get it right. Failing to comply with tax laws can result in penalties and fines, so let's break down what you need to know.

Sales Tax:

Sales tax is one of the most critical tax considerations for your dropshipping business. In the United States, sales tax is a state-level tax levied on the sale of products and services. The rules for collecting and remitting sales tax can vary significantly from state to state. Some states require you to collect sales tax if you have a physical presence (nexus) in the state, while others have economic nexus laws, meaning you need to collect sales tax if you exceed a certain amount of sales or transactions in the state.

To manage sales tax, you'll need to:

1. Register for a Sales Tax Permit: You'll need to register for a sales tax permit in each state where you have a nexus. This process usually entails filling out an application and paying a fee.

2. Collect Sales Tax: Once you have your permit, you need to start collecting sales tax from customers in those states. Most e-commerce platforms, including Shopify, have tools to help you calculate and collect the correct amount of sales tax at checkout.

3. Remit Sales Tax: Periodically, you'll need to remit the collected sales tax to the appropriate state authorities. This process usually involves filing a sales tax return, which reports your sales and the amount of sales tax collected.

Income Tax:

In addition to sales tax, you'll also need to pay income tax on the profits your business generates. The specifics of how you pay income tax depend on your business structure.

1. Sole Proprietorship and Partnerships: If you're a sole proprietor or a partner in a partnership, you'll report your business income on your personal tax return using Schedule C (Form 1040). Your business income will be subject to self-employment tax, which covers Social Security and Medicare taxes.

2. LLC: If you have an LLC, you can choose to be taxed as a sole proprietorship, partnership, or corporation. Single-member LLCs are automatically taxed as sole proprietorships, whereas multi-member LLCs are taxed as partnerships. However, you can elect to have your LLC taxed as a corporation by filing Form 8832 with the IRS.

3. Corporation: If your business is structured as a corporation, it will pay corporate income tax on its profits. Shareholders will also pay personal income tax on any dividends received, resulting in double taxation.

Estimated Taxes:

As a dropshipping business owner, you're responsible for paying estimated taxes throughout the year. These are quarterly tax payments made to the IRS and, in some cases, state tax authorities, to cover your income tax and self-employment tax.

The IRS expects you to pay at least 90% of your current year's tax liability or 100% of the previous year's tax liability, whichever is lower. Failure to make estimated tax payments can result in penalties and interest.

International Taxes:

If you sell to customers outside your home country, you'll need to understand and comply with international tax laws. Many countries require foreign businesses to collect and remit Value Added Tax (VAT) or Goods and Services Tax (GST) on sales to their residents. The rules and rates for these taxes can vary significantly, so it's essential to do your research and consult with a tax professional if needed.

Protecting Your Business: Terms and Conditions, Privacy Policies

To protect your dropshipping business, it's crucial to have clear and comprehensive terms and conditions and privacy policies. These documents help establish your business's legal framework, outline your responsibilities, and protect you from potential legal issues.

Terms and Conditions:

Your terms and conditions (T&C) are the rules that govern the use of your website and the purchase of your products. They set out the rights and responsibilities of both you and your customers and can help protect you from legal disputes. Here are some key elements to include in your T&C:

1. Introduction: Clearly state that the document outlines the terms and conditions for using your website and purchasing products from your store.

2. Definitions: Define key terms used throughout the document, such as "customer," "user," "we," and "you."

3. Acceptance of Terms: Specify that by using your website or making a purchase, customers agree to abide by your T&C.

4. Products and Services: Describe your products and services, including any limitations or restrictions.

5. Ordering and Payment: Outline the process for placing orders, accepted payment methods, and how payments are processed.

6. Shipping and Delivery: Detail your shipping and delivery policies, including shipping times, costs, and any potential delays.

7. Returns and Refunds: Explain your return and refund policy, including the conditions under which returns and refunds are accepted and the process for requesting them.

8. Intellectual Property: Assert your rights to any intellectual property on your website, such as logos, images, and content, and prohibit unauthorized use by customers.

9. *Limitation of Liability:* Limit your liability for any damages or losses resulting from the use of your website or products.

10. *Governing Law:* Specify the legal jurisdiction that will govern any disputes arising from your T&C.

Privacy Policies

A privacy policy is a document that explains how you collect, use, store, and protect your customers' personal information. Given the importance of data privacy in today's digital age, having a clear and transparent privacy policy is not only a legal requirement in many jurisdictions but also a way to build trust with your customers. Make sure your privacy policy has the following:

1. *Introduction:* Explain the purpose of the privacy policy and reassure customers that you are committed to protecting their privacy.

2. *Information Collection:* Detail what types of personal information you collect from customers, such as names, email addresses, shipping addresses, and payment information. Be specific about the methods of collection, whether through website forms, cookies, or third-party services.

3. *Use of Information:* Explain how you use the collected information. Common uses include processing orders, improving customer service, sending promotional emails, and conducting market research.

4. Information Sharing: Disclose whether you share customers' personal information with third parties, such as payment processors, shipping companies, and marketing partners. Ensure transparency about the circumstances under which information is shared and the types of third parties involved.

5. Data Protection: Describe the measures you take to protect customers' personal information from unauthorized access, disclosure, or misuse. This can include technical measures like encryption and secure servers, as well as administrative measures like access controls and staff training.

6. Customer Rights: Inform customers of their rights regarding their personal information, such as the right to access, correct, or delete their data. Explain the process for exercising these rights and provide contact information for customer inquiries.

7. Cookies and Tracking Technologies: Clarify your use of cookies and other tracking technologies on your website. Explain what cookies are, why you use them, and how customers may control their cookie settings.

8. Third-Party Links: If your website contains links to third-party websites, include a disclaimer that you are not responsible for the privacy practices of these external sites. Encourage customers to review the privacy policies of any linked websites.

9. Policy Changes: State that you may update your privacy policy from time to time and outline how customers will be notified of significant changes. Provide the date of the last update for transparency.

10. Contact Information: Provide a way for customers to contact you with questions or concerns about your privacy policy. This may be an email address, phone number, or contact form.

Implementing and Communicating Policies

Creating your terms and conditions and privacy policy is just the first step. You also need to implement these policies effectively and communicate them clearly to your customers.

- **Display Prominently:** Ensure that your terms and conditions and privacy policy are easily accessible on your website. Common places to display links to these documents include the footer of your website, the checkout page, and during the account registration process.

- **Customer Acceptance:** For your terms and conditions to be legally binding, customers must agree to them. You can achieve this by requiring customers to check a box indicating their acceptance of the terms before completing a purchase or creating an account.

- **Regular Updates:** Regularly review and update your terms and conditions and privacy policy to reflect changes in your business practices or legal requirements. Notify customers of significant updates and consider requiring them to accept the revised terms.

- Staff Training: Ensure that your staff understands your policies and knows how to handle customer inquiries related to terms and conditions and privacy practices. This is particularly important for customer service representatives who may need to address questions or concerns from customers.

Legal Support and Resources

Navigating the legal and financial requirements of a dropshipping business can be complex, and you don't have to do it alone. Here are some resources and support options to consider:

- Legal Professionals: Consider consulting with a lawyer who specializes in e-commerce or small business law. They can help you draft your terms and conditions, privacy policy, and other legal documents, as well as provide advice on compliance with local and international laws.

- Accountants and Tax Advisors: Working with an accountant or tax advisor can help you manage your tax obligations and ensure that your business is financially sound. They can assist with setting up your business structure, managing bookkeeping and accounting, and preparing tax returns.

- Online Resources: There are many online resources available to help you understand the legal and financial aspects of running a dropshipping business. Websites like the Small Business Administration (SBA) in the U.S., government portals for business registration and tax information, and e-commerce

platforms like Shopify often provide guides, templates, and support articles.

- *E-commerce Communities:* Joining e-commerce communities, such as online forums, social media groups, and local business networks, can provide valuable insights and support from fellow entrepreneurs. You can learn from others' experiences, ask questions, and share knowledge about best practices for legal and financial compliance.

Ensuring that your dropshipping business is legally compliant and financially sound is a critical aspect of building a successful and sustainable venture. When you understand the legal requirements, set up the right business entity, manage your tax obligations, and protect your business with clear terms and conditions and privacy policies, you can reduce risks and concentrate on expanding your business. Taking the time to address these legal and financial considerations upfront can save you from potential headaches and legal issues down the road. By doing so, you'll not only protect your business but also build trust with your customers and create a strong foundation for long-term success.

Managing Your Finances

Understanding and managing your finances is crucial to the success of your dropshipping business. It involves keeping track of your income and expenses, ensuring you have enough funds to cover your costs, and planning for future growth. Effective financial management can help you avoid cash flow problems, make informed business decisions, and achieve your financial goals.

Understanding Income and Expenses

The first step in managing your finances is understanding your income and expenses. Income refers to the money you receive from sales, while expenses are the costs you incur to run your business. Here's a closer look at each:

- **Income:** This includes the revenue from selling products on your Shopify store. It's essential to track your sales carefully to understand how much money your business is generating. You can use Shopify's built-in analytics tools to monitor your sales performance and identify trends.

- **Expenses:** Expenses can be divided into two main categories: fixed and variable. Fixed expenses are regular, ongoing costs that don't change much, such as your Shopify subscription, website hosting fees, and business insurance. Variable expenses fluctuate based on your sales volume and business activities, including product costs, shipping fees, marketing expenses, and transaction fees from payment gateways.

Tracking Your Finances:

To keep your finances in check, you'll need to track your income and expenses regularly. This can be done manually using spreadsheets or through accounting software. Here are a few steps to help you start:

1. Create a Budget: A budget is a financial plan that outlines your expected income and expenses over a specific period. Creating a budget helps you allocate resources effectively and ensures you have enough funds to cover your costs. We'll dive deeper into budgeting and financial planning later in this chapter.

2. Record Transactions: Keep a record of all your financial transactions, including sales, expenses, and payments. This helps you monitor your cash flow and provides a clear picture of your financial health. You can use tools like QuickBooks, Xero, or even Excel to track your transactions.

3. Reconcile Accounts: Regularly reconcile your accounts to ensure your records match your bank statements. This helps identify any discrepancies and ensures your financial data is accurate.

4. Analyze Financial Reports: Review your financial reports regularly to understand your business's performance. Key reports to monitor include your profit and loss statement, balance sheet, and cash flow statement. These reports provide information about your revenue, expenses, assets, liabilities, and overall financial situation.

Setting Up Payment Gateways

Setting up payment gateways is a crucial step in managing your finances and ensuring a smooth transaction process for your customers. A payment gateway is a service that processes credit card payments for online and offline businesses. It acts as an intermediary between your Shopify store and the payment processor, ensuring that transactions are completed securely and efficiently.

Choosing the Right Payment Gateway:

When selecting a payment gateway for your dropshipping business, consider the following factors:

- Compatibility with Shopify: Ensure the payment gateway you choose is compatible with Shopify. Shopify supports a wide range of payment gateways, including Shopify Payments, PayPal, Stripe, and more.

- Transaction Fees: The fees associated with using various payment channels vary. These fees can include a percentage of the transaction amount, a flat fee per transaction, or both. Compare the fees of different payment gateways to find one that offers a competitive rate.

- Supported Payment Methods: Consider the payment methods that the gateway accepts. The more options you provide, the more convenient it will be for your customers. Common payment methods include credit and debit cards, digital wallets like PayPal and Apple Pay, and alternative payment methods like bank transfers and cryptocurrency.

- Security: Security is crucial while handling online transactions. Choose a payment gateway that offers robust security features, such as encryption, fraud detection, and PCI compliance.

- Ease of Integration: The payment gateway should be easy to integrate with your Shopify store. Most major payment gateways offer plugins or apps that simplify the integration process.

Setting Up Payment Gateways on Shopify:

Once you've chosen a payment gateway, follow these steps to set it up on your Shopify store:

1. Access Payment Settings: Log in to your Shopify admin panel and navigate to Settings > Payments.

2. Select Payment Gateway: Under the "Payment providers" section, click on "Choose a provider" and select your preferred payment gateway from the list. If you're using Shopify Payments, you can activate it directly from this page.

3. Configure Payment Gateway: Follow the instructions to configure your payment gateway. This typically involves entering your account details, API keys, and other necessary information.

4. Test Transactions: Before going live, perform test transactions to ensure everything is working correctly. Most payment gateways have a sandbox or test mode for this cause.

5. Go Live: Once you've confirmed that the payment gateway is functioning correctly, switch to live mode and start accepting payments from your customers.

Budgeting and Financial Planning:

Effective budgeting and financial planning are essential for the long-term success of your dropshipping business. A well-crafted budget helps you allocate resources, control expenses, and plan for future growth. Financial planning involves setting financial goals, creating strategies to achieve them, and monitoring your progress.

1. Creating a Budget: Creating a budget involves estimating your income and expenses over a specific period, typically monthly or categories that represent different types of income, expenses, assets, liabilities, and equity. Common categories for a dropshipping business might include sales revenue, cost of goods sold, marketing expenses, shipping costs, and software subscriptions.

2. Record Transactions: Enter all your financial transactions into your accounting software. This includes sales, expenses, bank deposits, and withdrawals. Most accounting software allows you to connect your bank account and Shopify store for automatic transaction imports, saving you time and reducing errors.

3. Reconcile Accounts: Regularly reconcile your bank and credit card statements with your accounting records. This ensures that your records are accurate and helps identify any discrepancies or fraudulent transactions.

4. Generate Financial Reports: Use your accounting software to generate key financial reports, such as the profit and loss statement, balance sheet, and cash flow statement. These reports provide valuable insights into your business's financial health and help you make informed decisions.

Understanding Key Financial Reports:

To effectively manage your finances, it's essential to understand the key financial reports for your business. Here's a brief overview of the most important reports:

- *Profit and Loss Statement (P&L):* Also known as the income statement, the P&L shows your business's revenue, expenses, and net profit over a specific period. It helps you understand how much money you're making and where you're spending it.

- *Balance Sheet:* The balance sheet shows the financial status of your company as of a particular date. It lists your assets (what you own), liabilities (what you owe), and equity (the owner's interest in the business). This report helps you understand your business's financial stability and liquidity.

- *Cash Flow Statement:* The cash flow statement shows the inflows and outflows of cash over a specific period. It breaks down cash flow into three categories: operating activities, investing activities, and financing activities. This report helps you understand how cash moves through your business and identify potential cash flow issues.

Handling Taxes and Compliance:

Staying compliant with tax laws and regulations is a critical aspect of managing your dropshipping business's finances. Here are some key considerations for handling taxes and compliance:

*- **Sales Tax Compliance:*** As mentioned earlier, sales tax compliance is essential for dropshipping businesses. Ensure you're registered for sales tax permits in the states where you have a nexus, and regularly collect and remit sales tax to the appropriate authorities.

*- **Income Tax:*** Depending on your business structure, you'll need to report your business income on your personal or corporate tax return. Keep accurate records of your income and expenses to simplify tax preparation and ensure you're claiming all eligible deductions.

*- **Estimated Taxes:*** If you're self-employed or have significant business income, you may need to make quarterly estimated tax payments to the IRS and state tax authorities. These payments cover both your income tax and self-employment tax liabilities.

*- **Tax Deductions and Credits:*** Take advantage of available tax deductions and credits to reduce your tax liability. Common deductions for dropshipping businesses include home office expenses, internet and phone costs, software subscriptions, and business-related travel expenses.

*- **Consult a Tax Professional:*** Consider working with a tax professional or accountant to ensure you're compliant with tax laws and regulations. They can help you prepare and file your tax returns, identify tax-saving opportunities, and provide guidance on complex tax issues.

*** Financial Best Practices:***

Implementing financial best practices can help you manage your dropshipping business's finances more effectively and achieve long-term success. Here are some tips to keep in mind:

- ***Separate Business and Personal Finances:*** Keep your business and personal finances separate by opening a dedicated business bank account and credit card. This simplifies accounting and helps protect your personal assets.

- ***Create a Financial Plan:*** Develop a comprehensive financial plan that outlines your income goals, expense projections, and strategies for growth. Regularly review and update your plan to stay on track.

- ***Monitor Key Metrics:*** Track key financial metrics, such as gross profit margin, net profit margin, and customer acquisition cost. These metrics provide insights into your business's performance and help you make data-driven decisions.

- ***Build an Emergency Fund:*** Set aside funds in an emergency savings account to cover unexpected expenses or cash flow shortages. Aim to save at least three to six months' worth of operating expenses.

- ***Invest in Growth:*** Reinvest a portion of your profits into your business to fuel growth. This could include investing in marketing, expanding your product line, or upgrading your website and technology.

- ***Seek Professional Advice:*** Don't hesitate to seek advice from financial professionals, such as accountants, financial advisors, and business consultants. They can provide valuable insights and guidance to help you manage your finances more effectively.

Managing the legal and financial aspects of your dropshipping business is essential for long-term success. By understanding your income and expenses, setting up efficient payment gateways, creating a detailed budget, and implementing effective cash flow and accounting practices, you can keep your business financially healthy and in compliance with all necessary regulations.

Taking the time to properly manage your finances can save you from potential headaches and financial problems down the road. It also provides a solid foundation for growth and helps you make informed decisions that contribute to the success of your dropshipping business.

CHAPTER EIGHT

Key Challenges and How to Overcome Them

Like any entrepreneurial venture, dropshipping comes with its fair share of challenges. In this chapter, we'll go deep into these challenges and, more importantly, how you can overcome them. Remember, every obstacle is an opportunity in disguise, and with the right mindset and strategies, you can turn these challenges into stepping stones to success.

Challenge 1: Finding Reliable Suppliers

One of the biggest hurdles in dropshipping is finding reliable suppliers. Your business depends on them for inventory, timely shipping, and product quality. A bad supplier can lead to unhappy customers and damage your store's reputation.

How to Overcome It:

1. Research and Vet Suppliers:

- *Check Reviews:* Look for reviews and testimonials from other dropshippers. Platforms like AliExpress, Oberlo, and Spocket have reviews that can give you insights into a supplier's reliability.

- *Order Samples*: Request product samples before making a decision.

This allows you to check the quality firsthand and see how long the shipping takes.

   - **Communicate:** Reach out to potential suppliers and gauge their responsiveness. A good supplier will be prompt and clear in their communication.

2. Use Multiple Suppliers:

   - Don't put all your eggs in one basket. Using multiple suppliers can mitigate the risk if one fails to deliver.

3. Build Relationships:

   - Establishing a good relationship with your suppliers can lead to better deals, priority shipping, and quicker resolutions to issues.

Challenge 2: Managing Customer Expectations

Managing customer expectations is crucial in dropshipping, especially since you don't control the inventory or the shipping process directly.

How to Overcome It:

1. Clear Communication:

   - **Shipping Times:** Be transparent about shipping times on your product pages. Dropshipping often involves longer shipping times, and it's essential your customers know this upfront.

- Product Descriptions: Make sure your product descriptions are exact and detailed. Misleading descriptions can lead to returns and unhappy customers.

2. Proactive Customer Service:

   - Respond Swiftly: Strive to respond to customer inquiries within 24 hours. Prompt responses can turn a potential issue into a positive customer experience.

   - Follow Up: After a purchase, follow up with customers to confirm they received their product and are satisfied.

3. Set Realistic Expectations:

   - Under-promise and over-deliver. It's better to tell customers their order will take 15 days and have it arrive in 10 than the other way around.

Challenge 3: Handling Returns and Refunds

Returns and refunds are part of any retail business, but they can be particularly challenging in dropshipping due to the logistics involved.

How to Overcome It:

1. Clear Return Policy:

   - Simple and Transparent: Make sure your return policy is easy to understand and accessible on your website.

   - Reasonable Time Frame: Offer a reasonable time frame for returns (e.g., 30 days).

2. Efficient Processes:

  - *Automate:* Use Shopify apps that can help automate the return process, making it easier for both you and your customers.

  - *Work with Suppliers:* Ensure your suppliers have a return policy and understand their terms.

3. Customer-Centric Approach:

  - *Be Flexible:* Sometimes, it's worth going the extra mile for a customer, even if it means bending your return policy slightly. As customer who is satisfied is more likely to come back.

Challenge 4: Competition and Pricing Wars

The dropshipping market is highly competitive. You may find yourself competing with numerous other stores selling the same or similar products.

How to Overcome It:

1. Niche Down:

  - *Find Your Niche:* Instead of selling generic products, focus on a specific niche. This can help you target a more specific audience and reduce competition.

  - *Unique Selling Proposition (USP):* Identify what distinguishes your store. It could be your product selection, customer service, or branding.

2. Value Over Price:

- **Build Brand Loyalty:** Offer value through quality content, excellent customer service, and a strong brand identity. Customers are generally willing to spend more for a brand they know and trust.

- **Bundling and Upselling:** Offer product bundles or upsell complementary products to increase the average order value.

3. Marketing Strategies:

- **SEO:** Optimize your store for search engines to generate organic visitors.

- **Social Media:** Use social media to create a community for your brand. Engaging content and regular interaction can help you stand out.

Challenge 5: Managing Cash Flow

Cash flow management is crucial in any business. In dropshipping, it can be particularly tricky since you need to pay your suppliers before receiving payment from your customers.

How to Overcome It:

1. Budgeting and Forecasting:

- **Track Expenses:** Keep a close eye on your expenses and budget accordingly.

- Sales Forecasting: Use historical data to forecast sales and plan for peak periods.

2. Payment Gateways:

- Multiple Gateways: Use multiple payment gateways to ensure you receive funds quickly and reduce the risk of payment issues.

- Advance Payments: Consider asking for advance payments for large orders.

3. Credit Options:

- Business Credit Card: Use a business credit card for supplier payments to manage cash flow better and earn rewards.

- Short-Term Loans: Explore short-term financing options if needed, but use them wisely to avoid debt.

Challenge 6: Staying Updated with Market Trends

The e-commerce and dropshipping landscape is constantly evolving. Staying updated with market trends is essential to remain competitive and meet customer demands.

How to Overcome It:

1. Continuous Learning:

- Online Courses and Webinars: Invest in your education by taking online courses and attending webinars on e-commerce and digital marketing.

- Industry Blogs and Podcasts: Follow industry blogs and podcasts to stay informed about the latest trends and best practices.

2. Customer Feedback:

- Surveys and Reviews: Regularly seek feedback from your customers through surveys and reviews. Their insights can help you improve and adapt to their needs.

- Engagement: Engage with your customers on social media and through email marketing to understand their preferences and expectations.

3. Competitor Analysis:

- Monitor Competitors: Keep an eye on your competitors to see what they are doing well and identify areas where you can differentiate yourself.

- Benchmarking: Use competitor analysis tools to benchmark your performance against industry standards.

Challenge 7: Building Trust and Credibility

Trust and credibility are crucial in e-commerce. Since customers cannot physically inspect the products, they need to trust that they will receive what they ordered.

How to Overcome It:

1. Professional Website:

- *Design and Usability:* Invest in a professional website design that is easy to navigate and visually appealing.

- *Trust Signals:* Display trust signals such as secure payment icons, customer reviews, and trust badges.

2. Customer Reviews and Testimonials:

- *Collect and Display:* Actively collect and display customer reviews and testimonials on your website.

- *Respond to Reviews:* Respond to both positive and negative reviews to show that you value customer feedback.

3. Transparency:

- *About Us Page:* Create a compelling "About Us" page that tells your brand story and builds a connection with your customers.

- *Clear Policies:* Ensure that your shipping, return, and privacy policies are clear and easy to find.

Challenge 8: Scaling Your Business

Scaling your dropshipping business can be challenging, especially as you need to manage increased orders, customer service, and marketing efforts.

How to Overcome It:

1. Automation:

   - ***Tools and Apps:*** Use automation tools and apps to streamline order processing, inventory management, and customer service.

   - ***Email Marketing:*** Automate your email marketing campaigns to nurture leads and drive repeat purchases.

2. Outsourcing:

   - ***Virtual Assistants:*** Hire virtual assistants to handle repetitive tasks such as customer support and order processing.

   - ***Freelancers:*** Work with freelancers for specialized tasks such as graphic design, content creation, and social media management.

3. Efficient Operations:

   - ***Standard Operating Procedures (SOPs):*** Create SOPs for your business processes to ensure consistency and efficiency.

   - ***Performance Metrics:*** Track key performance metrics to identify areas for improvement and measure your progress.

Challenge 9: Legal and Compliance Issues

Navigating legal and compliance issues can be complex in dropshipping, especially when dealing with international suppliers and customers.

How to Overcome It:

1. Research and Understand Regulations:

   - **Local and International Laws:** Research the laws and regulations that apply to your business, both locally and internationally.

   - **Taxes and Duties:** Understand the tax and duty implications of selling to different countries.

2. Professional Advice:

   - **Legal and Accounting Experts:** Consult with legal and accounting professionals to ensure your business is compliant with all relevant regulations.

   - **Terms and Conditions:** Create clear terms and conditions, privacy policy, and other legal documents for your website.

3. Protect Your Business:

   - **Insurance:** Consider getting business insurance to protect against potential liabilities and risks.

   - **Intellectual Property:** Protect your intellectual property by trademarking your brand and products where applicable.

Challenge 10: Dealing with Fraud and Chargebacks

Fraud and chargebacks can be significant issues in e-commerce, leading to financial losses and potential damage to your business reputation.

How to Overcome It:

1. Fraud Prevention Measures:

- *Secure Payment Gateways:* Use trusted and secure payment gateways that offer fraud protection features.

- *Verification Steps:* Implement additional verification steps, such as address verification and CVV checks, to reduce fraudulent transactions.

2. Monitor Transactions:

- *Regular Monitoring:* Regularly monitor transactions for any suspicious activity. Look for red flags such as mismatched billing and shipping addresses or unusually large orders.

- *Fraud Detection Tools:* Utilize fraud detection tools and services that can help identify and prevent fraudulent transactions.

3. Clear Refund Policies:

- *Detailed Policies:* Clearly outline your refund and chargeback policies on your website to set customer expectations.

- *Dispute Management:* Be prepared to manage and dispute chargebacks effectively. Keep thorough records of transactions and communication with customers to support your case if needed.

Challenge 11: Maintaining Work-Life Balance

Running a dropshipping business can be time-consuming and demanding, making it challenging to maintain a healthy work-life balance.

How to Overcome It:

1. Time Management:

  - **Set Priorities:** Prioritize tasks based on their importance and urgency. Concentrate on high-impact activities that promote growth.

  - **Use Tools:** Use productivity tools and apps to manage your time effectively and stay organized.

2. Delegation:

  - **Delegate Tasks:** Delegate tasks to team members or outsource tasks to freelancers and virtual assistants. Focus on the strategic aspects of your business while others handle routine tasks.

  - **Create Systems:** Develop systems and processes that allow your business to run smoothly even when you're not directly involved.

3. Self-Care:

-**Set Boundaries:** Define clear boundaries between work and personal time. Schedule regular breaks and downtime to refuel.

  - **Healthy Habits:** Maintain healthy habits such as regular exercise, proper nutrition, and sufficient sleep to stay energized and focused.

Challenge 12: Adapting to Technological Changes

The technology landscape is constantly evolving, and staying up-to-date with the latest tools and trends can be challenging but essential for your business's success.

How to Overcome It:

1. Continuous Learning:

- ***Stay Informed:*** Follow industry blogs, attend webinars, and participate in online forums to stay informed about the latest technological advancements.

- ***Online Courses:*** Enroll in online courses and training programs to enhance your skills and knowledge in e-commerce and digital marketing.

2. Experimentation:

- ***Test New Tools:*** Don't be afraid to test new tools and technologies that could streamline your operations or enhance your customer experience.

- ***Analyze Results:*** Continuously analyze the results of your experiments to determine what works best for your business.

3. Network with Peers:

- ***Join Communities:*** Join e-commerce and dropshipping communities to network with peers, share experiences, and learn from others.

- ***Attend Events:*** Attend industry conferences and events to connect with experts and stay updated on the latest trends and technologies.

Challenge 13: Marketing Effectively

Effective marketing is crucial to attract customers and drive sales. However, with so many marketing channels available, it can be overwhelming to determine where to focus your efforts.

How to Overcome It:

1. Understand Your Audience:

 - *Customer Personas:* Develop detailed customer personas to understand your target audience's needs, preferences, and behaviors.

 - *Market Research*: Conduct market research to gather insights into your audience and competitors.

2. Multi-Channel Approach:

-Diversify Your Channels: Don't rely on just one marketing channel. Use a combination of channels such as social media, email marketing, SEO, and paid advertising to reach a broader audience.

 - *Consistent Branding:* Ensure consistent branding and messaging across all marketing channels to build brand recognition and trust.

3. Analyze and Optimize:

 - *Track Performance:* Use analytics tools to track the performance of your marketing campaigns and identify what works best.

*- **Continuous Improvement:*** Continuously optimize your marketing strategies based on data and feedback to improve results and ROI.

Challenge 14: Inventory Management

Although you don't hold physical inventory in dropshipping, managing inventory effectively is still crucial to ensure product availability and prevent stockouts.

How to Overcome It:

1. Sync with Suppliers:

*- **Real-Time Updates:*** Use tools that sync your store with your suppliers' inventory to get real-time updates on stock levels.

*- **Alert Systems:*** Set up alert systems to notify you when stock levels are low or when products are back in stock.

2. Product Range Management:

*- **Analyze Sales Data:*** Regularly analyze sales data to identify best-selling products and focus on promoting them.

*- **Seasonal Trends:*** Pay attention to seasonal trends and adjust your product range accordingly to meet customer demand.

3. Backup Suppliers:

*- **Multiple Sources:*** Have backup suppliers for your best-selling products to ensure continuous availability.

- Regular Communication: Maintain regular communication with your suppliers to stay informed about inventory levels and potential issues.

Challenge 15: Building a Strong Brand

In a competitive market, building a strong brand that resonates with your target audience is essential for differentiation and long-term success.

How to Overcome It:

1. Brand Identity:

- Define Your Brand: Clearly outline your brand's mission, vision, values, and unique selling proposition.

- Visual Identity: Create a consistent visual identity for your brand, including a logo, color scheme, and typography that reflects its personality.

2. Consistent Messaging:

- Voice and Tone: Establish a consistent brand voice and tone across all communication channels.

- Storytelling: Use storytelling to connect with your audience on an emotional level and build a strong brand narrative.

3. Customer Experience:

- Exceptional Service: Provide exceptional customer service at every touchpoint to build trust and loyalty.

- Brand Ambassadors: Encourage satisfied customers to become brand ambassadors by sharing their positive experiences and reviews.

Dropshipping on Shopify is a journey filled with challenges, but each challenge presents an opportunity for growth and improvement. By proactively addressing these challenges and implementing the strategies outlined in this chapter, you can navigate the dropshipping landscape more effectively and build a successful online business. Remember, perseverance and adaptability are key. Embrace the learning process, stay committed to your goals, and continue to refine your approach as you gain more experience.

CHAPTER NINE
Future Trends and Strategies

Adapting to Changing E-commerce Trends

E-commerce is a dynamic field, and the ability to adapt to new trends is a significant factor in your success. Here are some key trends you should keep an eye on and strategies to help you adapt.

Trend 1: The Rise of Mobile Commerce

Far more people are shopping and making purchases on their smartphones than ever before. Mobile commerce, or m-commerce, is a trend that's here to stay.

How to Adapt:

1. Mobile-First Design:

  - Ensure your Shopify store is mobile-friendly. Use responsive design to ensure that your website looks excellent and works properly on all devices.

  - Simplify navigation and minimize loading times to enhance the mobile shopping experience.

2. Mobile Payment Options:

  - Integrate mobile payment options like Apple Pay, Google Pay, and other digital wallets to make checkout seamless for mobile users.

3. Optimize for Voice Search:

- With the rise of voice assistants, optimizing your store for voice search can help capture more mobile traffic. Use natural language and long-tail keywords in your product descriptions and FAQs.

Trend 2: Personalization and Customer Experience

Personalized shopping experiences are becoming the norm. Customers expect retailers to understand their preferences and offer tailored recommendations.

How to Adapt:

1. Data-Driven Personalization:

- Use customer data to personalize product recommendations, email marketing campaigns, and targeted ads.

- Segment your audience based on their behavior, preferences, and purchase history to deliver relevant content.

2. AI and Machine Learning:

- Leverage AI and machine learning tools to analyze customer data and automate personalization at scale.

- Implement chatbots to provide personalized customer support and improve response times.

3. Enhanced Customer Experience:

- Focus on providing a great customer experience at all touchpoints. From easy navigation to quick support, every aspect of your store should prioritize the customer.

Trend 3: Sustainable and Ethical Shopping

Consumers are increasingly conscious of their impact on the environment and are seeking sustainable and ethically-sourced products.

How to Adapt:

1. Sustainable Products:

- Source and offer eco-friendly and sustainable products. Include these products in your store and marketing materials.

- Work with suppliers who adhere to ethical practices and environmental standards.

2. Transparency:

- Be transparent about your sourcing and manufacturing processes. Share your sustainability efforts and certifications with your customers.

- Use clear and honest communication to build trust with your audience.

3. Reduce Carbon Footprint:

- Offer carbon-neutral shipping options and consider offsetting your carbon footprint through initiatives like tree planting or renewable energy investments.

- Encourage customers to make environmentally-friendly choices with incentives for choosing sustainable products or shipping options.

Trend 4: Social Commerce

Social media platforms are becoming powerful sales channels, with features like shoppable posts and integrated checkouts.

How to Adapt:

1. Shoppable Posts:

- Use platforms like Instagram and Facebook to create shoppable posts that allow customers to purchase products directly from your social media profiles.

- Regularly update your social media accounts with engaging content and product showcases.

2. Live Shopping:

- Experiment with live shopping events on platforms like Facebook Live or Instagram Live. Showcase your products in real-time and interact with your audience to drive sales.

- Use live streams to demonstrate product features, answer questions, and offer exclusive deals.

Exploring New Opportunities and Platforms

As the e-commerce landscape evolves, new opportunities and platforms emerge. Staying open to these possibilities can help you expand your business and reach new markets.

Opportunity 1: Expanding to International Markets

Global e-commerce is growing, and expanding to international markets can significantly increase your customer base.

How to Explore:

1. Localized Websites:

  - Create localized versions of your Shopify store to cater to different regions. Translate your website and product descriptions to the local language.

  - Customize your marketing strategies to fit the cultural and buying preferences of each market.

2. International Shipping:

  - Partner with reliable international shipping providers to ensure timely delivery.

  - Clearly communicate shipping times, costs, and any potential customs fees to international customers.

3. Market Research:

- Conduct thorough market research to identify high-potential regions and understand local competitors.

- Tailor your product offerings to meet the needs and preferences of international customers.

Opportunity 2: Embracing Emerging Technologies

Staying ahead of technological advancements can give you a competitive edge and improve your operational efficiency.

How to Explore:

1. Augmented Reality (AR):

- Implement AR features to allow customers to visualize products in their environment before purchasing.

- Use AR for virtual try-ons, especially for fashion and accessories, to enhance the shopping experience.

2. Blockchain Technology:

- Explore the use of blockchain for supply chain transparency and secure transactions.

- Blockchain can enhance trust by providing verifiable information about product origins and manufacturing processes.

3. Artificial Intelligence (AI):

- Use AI-powered tools for inventory management, demand forecasting, and customer service automation.

- Implement AI chatbots to provide instant support and personalized recommendations to customers.

Opportunity 3: Subscription-Based Models

Subscription-based models can provide a steady revenue stream and increase customer retention.

How to Explore:

1. Subscription Boxes:

- Offer curated subscription boxes that deliver a selection of products to customers on a regular basis.

- Personalize subscription boxes based on customer preferences and past purchases.

2. Membership Programs:

- Create membership programs that offer exclusive benefits, such as discounts, early access to new products, and free shipping.

- Encourage customers to join by highlighting the value and savings they'll receive.

3. Automated Reordering:

- Implement automated reordering options for consumable products. Allow customers to set up recurring orders for items they regularly purchase.

- Provide incentives, such as discounts or free shipping, for customers who opt for automated reordering.

Opportunity 4: Diversifying Sales Channels

It can be unsafe to rely just on one sales channel. Diversifying your sales channels can help you reach a broader audience and reduce dependency on any one platform.

How to Explore:

1. Marketplaces:

  - List your products on popular marketplaces like Amazon, eBay, and Etsy to reach more customers.

  - Optimize your product listings for each marketplace to improve visibility and sales.

2. Social Media:

  - Sell directly on social media platforms using their integrated shopping features.

  - Use social media ads to drive traffic to your store and increase conversions.

3. Physical Pop-Up Shops:

  - Consider setting up physical pop-up shops or participating in local markets to create a tangible shopping experience.

  - Use these opportunities to connect with customers in person and build brand awareness.

Opportunity 5: Leveraging Data Analytics

Data is a powerful tool for making informed decisions and improving your business strategies.

How to Explore:

1. Customer Insights:

  - Use data analytics tools to gather insights into customer behavior, preferences, and purchase patterns.

  - Segment your audience based on data to create targeted marketing campaigns and personalized experiences.

2. Sales Performance:

  - Analyze sales data to identify trends, best-selling products, and areas for improvement.

  - Use this information to optimize your inventory, pricing, and marketing strategies.

Conclusion

As the dropshipping world continues to evolve, staying informed and adaptable is key to sustaining and growing your business. By embracing new trends and exploring emerging opportunities, you can position yourself for long-term success in the competitive e-commerce market. Remember, the future of dropshipping is bright, and with the right strategies, you can navigate the changes and thrive in this dynamic industry. Keep learning, experimenting, and innovating to stay ahead of the curve and build a resilient and profitable dropshipping business.

CHAPTER TEN

How to Succeed in Your Dropshipping Business

Vetting Your Copywriter

Your copywriter is instrumental in conveying your brand message, engaging your audience, and driving sales. Here's how to make sure you find the ideal person for the job:

Understanding the Role of a Copywriter

A copywriter creates the text for your website, product descriptions, email campaigns, ads, and more. Their words can make or break your sales pitch.

Key Responsibilities:

- **Product Descriptions:** Crafting persuasive and informative product descriptions that highlight features and benefits.

- **Website Copy:** Writing engaging content for your homepage, about page, and other key sections of your site.

- **Marketing Materials:** Creating compelling copy for email marketing, social media, and ad campaigns.

- SEO Optimization: Ensuring content is optimized for search engines to drive organic traffic.

Finding Potential Copywriters

To find a skilled copywriter, you need to know where to look and what to look for.

Where to Find Copywriters:

- Freelance Platforms: Websites like Upwork, Freelancer, and Fiverr have numerous freelance copywriters available for hire.

- Content Agencies: Consider working with content agencies that specialize in e-commerce copywriting.

- Professional Networks: LinkedIn and other professional networks can be excellent places to find experienced copywriters.

- Referrals: Ask for recommendations from your network or other e-commerce entrepreneurs.

Evaluating Copywriters

Once you have a list of potential candidates, it's time to evaluate their suitability for your business.

Portfolio Review:

- Relevance: Look for examples of their work that are relevant to e-commerce and your specific niche.

- Quality: Assess the quality of their writing. Is it engaging, clear, and persuasive? Does it match the tone you want for your brand?

- Results: Check if their copy has driven results, such as increased sales or engagement.

Skills and Expertise:

- SEO Knowledge: Ensure they understand SEO principles and can optimize content for search engines.

- Marketing Savvy: A good copywriter should have a solid grasp of marketing principles and how to appeal to your target audience.

- Adaptability: They should be able to adapt their writing style to match your brand's voice and tone.

Trial Project:

- Sample Work: Consider asking them to complete a small paid trial project. This could be a product description or a short blog post.

- Feedback: Provide feedback on their trial work and see how they respond. Are they open to revisions and suggestions?

Communication:

*- **Responsiveness:*** Assess their communication skills. Are they receptive and simple to get in touch with?

*- **Professionalism:*** Look for professionalism in their emails and interactions. This can be indicative of their work ethic.

Vetting Your Designer

A skilled designer can make your store visually appealing and user-friendly. Here's how to find the right designer for your dropshipping business.

Understanding the Role of a Designer

A designer is responsible for the visual elements of your store, including the layout, color scheme, typography, and overall aesthetic.

Key Responsibilities:

*- **Website Design:*** Creating a visually appealing and functional website layout.

*- **Brand Identity:*** Designing your logo, color palette, and other branding elements.

*- **Product Imagery:*** Enhancing product images and creating graphics for your store.

- User Experience (UX): Ensuring the site is easy to navigate and provides a positive user experience.

Finding Potential Designers

Finding a talented designer involves knowing where to look and what qualifications to seek.

Where to Find Designers:

- Freelance Platforms: Upwork, Freelancer, and Fiverr have many freelance designers available for hire.

- Design Agencies: Consider hiring a design agency that specializes in e-commerce design.

- Design Communities: Websites like Behance and Dribbble showcase portfolios of talented designers.

- Referrals: Ask for recommendations from your network or other e-commerce entrepreneurs.

Evaluating Designers

Once you have potential candidates, it's crucial to evaluate their suitability.

Portfolio Review:

- Relevance: Look for work that is relevant to e-commerce and your specific niche.

- Quality: Evaluate the quality of their design work.

Is it visually appealing and professional? Does it match the style you want for your brand?

- **Functionality:** Check if their designs are not only attractive but also functional and user-friendly.

Skills and Expertise:

- **E-commerce Experience:** Ensure they have experience designing for e-commerce stores.

- **Technical Skills:** Verify their proficiency in design tools like Adobe Creative Suite, Sketch, or Figma.

- **UX/UI Knowledge:** They should have a solid understanding of user experience (UX) and user interface (UI) design principles.

Trial Project:

- **Sample Work:** Consider asking them to complete a small paid trial project. This could be a homepage mockup or a product page design.

- **Feedback:** Provide feedback on their trial work and see how they respond. Are they open to revisions and suggestions?

Communication:

- *Responsiveness:* Assess their communication skills. Are they receptive and simple to get in touch with?

- *Professionalism:* Look for professionalism in their emails and interactions. This can be indicative of their work ethic.

Adding Value to Your Business

Adding value to your dropshipping business is essential for standing out in a competitive market. Here's how you can enhance your business and provide exceptional value to your customers:

1. Unique Value Proposition (UVP)

Your unique value proposition sets you apart from competitors and gives customers a compelling reason to buy from you.

How to Create a Strong UVP:

- *Identify Your Strengths:* Determine what makes your products or services unique. This could be quality, price, customer service, or a unique feature.

- *Understand Your Audience:* Be familiar with your target audience's needs, preferences, and pain points. Tailor your UVP to address these.

- *Clear and Concise Messaging:* Communicate your UVP clearly and concisely on your website and marketing materials.

Example":

- If you sell environmentally friendly products, your unique selling point could be: "Sustainable products that don't cost the earth."

"Shop our eco-friendly range and make a difference with every purchase."

2. Exceptional Customer Service

Providing exceptional customer service can significantly enhance the customer experience and foster loyalty.

Strategies for Excellent Customer Service:

- **Responsive Support:** Provide prompt and helpful responses to customer inquiries. Aim to respond within 24 hours.

- **Multichannel Support:** Provide support through various channels like email, live chat, and social media.

- **Personalized Service:** Personalize interactions with customers by addressing them by name and referencing their previous purchases.

Example:

-Implement a live chat function on your website to help customers in real time.

 - Train your support team to handle queries effectively and empathetically.

3. High-Quality Products

Ensuring your products are of high quality can lead to satisfied customers and repeat business.

Ensuring Product Quality:

- **Supplier Vetting:** Thoroughly vet your suppliers to ensure they provide high-quality products.

- **Quality Control:** Regularly order samples and inspect them for quality. Conduct random quality checks on batches of products.

- **Customer Feedback:** Encourage customers to provide feedback and use it to improve product quality.

Example:

- Offer a satisfaction guarantee that allows customers to return products if they're not satisfied with the quality. This shows confidence in your products and builds trust.

4. User-Friendly Website

A user-friendly website enhances the shopping experience and increases the likelihood of conversions.

Improving Website Usability:

- **Simple Navigation:** Use a simple menu layout to make your website easier to navigate.

*- **Fast Loading Times:*** Optimize your site for speed to reduce bounce rates and improve user experience.

*- **Mobile Optimization:*** Make sure your website is fully responsive and performs well on mobile devices.

Example:

- Conduct regular usability testing to identify and fix any navigation issues. Use tools like Google Page Speed Insights to improve loading times.

5. Engaging Content

Creating engaging content can attract and retain customers, providing value beyond just the products you sell.

Types of Engaging Content:

*- **Blog Posts:*** Write informative and relevant blog posts related to your niche.

*- **Videos:*** Create product demonstration videos, tutorials, and behind-the-scenes content.

*- **User-Generated Content:*** Encourage customers to share their product-related experiences and feature their content on your website and social media channels.

Example:

- Start a blog that offers tips, guides, and trends related to your niche. For instance, if you're selling fitness equipment, write posts about workout routines, nutrition tips, and fitness trends.

6. Building a Community

Building a community around your brand can increase loyalty and promotion via word-of-mouth.

Strategies for Building a Community:

- *Social Media Engagement:* Actively interact with your target audience via your social media channels. Respond to comments, share user-generated content, and create members to foster a sense of exclusivity and belonging.

7. Leveraging Customer Feedback

Using customer feedback to improve your products and services can significantly enhance customer satisfaction and loyalty.

How to Gather and Use Feedback:

- *Surveys:* Regularly send out surveys to gather detailed feedback on customer experiences.

- *Product Reviews:* Encourage customers to leave reviews and read through them to identify common issues or praise.

- *Direct Communication:* Reach out to customers directly for feedback, especially after resolving an issue or making a sale.

Example:

- After a purchase, send a follow-up email asking for feedback on the product and the shopping experience. Use this feedback to make informed decisions on product improvements and service enhancements.

8. Implementing Effective Marketing Strategies

Effective marketing is essential for driving traffic, building brand awareness, and increasing sales.

Marketing Strategies to Consider:

- Content Marketing: Create intriguing contents that draws in and keeps the interest of your target audience. These may include Infographics, videos, blog entries, and more.

- Email Marketing: Build and nurture your email list with regular newsletters, promotional offers, and personalized recommendations.

- Social Media Marketing: Maintain an active presence on social media platforms where your target audience spends time. Post engaging content, run ads, and interact with followers.

Example:

- Develop a content calendar for your blog and social media channels. Plan out regular posts that provide value to your audience, such as how-to guides, industry news, and user-generated content.

9. Providing Excellent Post-Purchase Support

Excellent post-purchase support can turn a one-time buyer into a loyal customer.

How to Offer Excellent Post-Purchase Support:

- **Order Tracking:** Provide clear tracking information and updates on the status of orders.

- **Follow-Up Emails:** Send follow-up emails after a purchase to ensure customer satisfaction and offer assistance if needed.

- **Easy Returns and Exchanges:** Make the return and exchange process simple and hassle-free.

Example:

- Implement an automated email sequence that sends customers a thank-you email after their purchase, followed by a shipping update and a feedback request once the product is delivered.

Success in your dropshipping business requires careful attention to detail and a commitment to excellence in every aspect of your operations. By vetting your copywriter and designer, you ensure that your brand message is compelling and your website is visually appealing. Adding value to your business through a strong UVP, exceptional customer service, high-quality products, a user-friendly website, engaging content, community building, leveraging feedback, effective marketing, and excellent post-purchase support sets you apart from the competition.

Remember, the journey to success is ongoing. Continuously seek ways to improve, adapt to changing trends, and listen to your customers. With dedication and the right strategies, you can build a thriving dropshipping business that stands the test of time.

CHAPTER ELEVEN
Best Countries to Dropship from

Choosing the right countries to dropship from can significantly impact your business's success. Factors like shipping times, product quality, and supplier reliability vary from country to country. Here are some of the best countries to consider and why they are advantageous.

1. China:

China is a leading hub for dropshipping due to its vast manufacturing capabilities and extensive product range.

Advantages:

- Wide Product Range: China offers an unparalleled variety of products across virtually all categories.

- Cost-Effective: Products from China are often cheaper due to lower manufacturing costs.

- Established Suppliers: Many suppliers in China are experienced in dropshipping and understand the requirements of international shipping.

What You Need to Know:

- **Shipping Times:** Shipping from China can take longer, especially with standard shipping options. Consider offering expedited shipping for customers willing to pay extra.

- **Quality Control:** Not all suppliers are equal. Vet suppliers carefully and order samples to ensure product quality.

- **Customs and Duties:** Customs and Duties: Research the laws governing customs and levies in the markets you intend to target. Inform your customers about potential additional costs.

2. United States:

Dropshipping from the United States can be beneficial if your primary market is also in the U.S. or other nearby regions.

Advantages:

- **Faster Shipping:** Shipping within the U.S. is generally faster compared to international shipping.

- **Quality Assurance:** Products from U.S. suppliers often meet higher quality standards.

- **Customer Trust:** Many customers trust products that are shipped from within their own country.

What You Need to Know:

- **Higher Costs:** Products from U.S. suppliers may be more expensive due to higher manufacturing and labor costs.

- *Limited Range:* The variety of products may be more limited compared to countries like China.

- *Supplier Availability:* There are fewer dropshipping suppliers in the U.S. compared to China, making it essential to thoroughly vet potential suppliers.

3. Europe:

Europe, including countries like Germany, the UK, and the Netherlands, is another excellent region for dropshipping.

Advantages:

- *Quality Products:* European suppliers often offer high-quality products that meet strict regulatory standards.

- *Fast Shipping:* Shipping within Europe is generally fast, making it an excellent option if your target market is in Europe.

- *Customer Trust:* European customers tend to trust products shipped from within the region.

What You Need to Know:

- *Higher Prices:* Products from European suppliers can be more expensive due to higher production costs.

- *Language Barriers:* Be prepared to deal with language barriers when communicating with suppliers in non-English speaking countries.

- Customs and Regulations: Ensure you understand the customs regulations and VAT requirements for each European country you plan to ship to.

4. Australia:

Australia is a good option for dropshipping, especially if your target market includes Australia and New Zealand.

Advantages:

- **Quality Assurance:** Australian suppliers often provide high-quality products.

- **Faster Shipping:** Shipping within Australia and to New Zealand is relatively fast.

- **Customer Trust:** Australian customers trust products sourced from within their region.

What You Need to Know:

- **Higher Costs:** Products from Australian suppliers can be more expensive.

- **Limited Suppliers:** There are fewer dropshipping suppliers in Australia compared to other regions.

- **Geographical Distance:** If shipping to other parts of the world, the geographical distance can result in longer shipping times.

What You Need to Know About International Dropshipping

International dropshipping opens up a vast potential market, but it also involves complexities that domestic dropshipping doesn't. Here's what you need to know to navigate the world of international dropshipping successfully:

1. Understanding International Shipping

Shipping is a critical component of dropshipping. Here's what you need to consider when dealing with international shipping:

Shipping Methods:

- ***Standard Shipping:*** Economical but can take longer. Suitable for customers who are not in a rush.

- ***Expedited Shipping:*** Faster but more expensive. Offer this option for customers willing to pay extra for quicker delivery.

- ***Courier Services***: Services like DHL, FedEx, and UPS provide reliable and fast shipping options but come at a higher cost.

Shipping Costs:

- Variable Costs: Shipping costs can vary significantly based on destination, weight, and shipping method.

- *Incorporate Costs:* Decide whether to absorb shipping costs into your product pricing or charge customers separately.

Tracking and Reliability:

- *Trackable Shipping:* Always use shipping methods that offer tracking to keep customers informed about their order status.

- *Supplier Reliability:* Ensure your suppliers use reliable shipping services to minimize delivery issues.

2. Managing Customs and Duties

Customs and duties are essential considerations when shipping internationally. Here's how to manage them:

Customs Regulations:

- *Research:* Understand the customs regulations of the countries you're shipping to. Rules and regulations differ from country to country.

- *Documentation:* Ensure all shipments include the necessary customs documentation to avoid delays.

Duties and Taxes:

- Inform Customers: Clearly inform customers about potential customs duties and taxes they may need to pay upon delivery.

- Duties Paid: Decide whether you will cover the duties (Delivered Duty Paid - DDP) or if the customer will be responsible (Delivered Duty Unpaid - DDU).

Handling Returns:

- Return Policy: Establish a clear return policy for international orders, considering the potential complications and costs of international returns.

- Local Returns: Consider using a local returns address or service in key markets to simplify the return process for international customers.

4. Navigating Currency and Payment Gateways

Handling different currencies and payment gateways is crucial for a smooth international dropshipping operation.

Multiple Currencies:

- Currency Conversion: Offer prices in local currencies to improve customer experience and reduce cart abandonment.

- Payment Gateway Support: Ensure your payment gateway supports multiple currencies and international transactions.

Payment Gateways:

- ***Global Gateways:*** Use payment gateways that are widely accepted globally, such as PayPal, Stripe, and Shopify Payments.

- ***Localized Options:*** Offer localized payment methods popular in specific regions, such as Alipay in China or Klarna in Europe.

Exchange Rates:

- ***Regular Updates:*** Keep an eye on exchange rates and adjust your pricing accordingly to maintain profitability.

- ***Fees:*** Be aware of any additional fees charged by payment gateways for currency conversion and international transactions.

5. Adapting to Local Markets

Understanding and adapting to local markets can significantly impact your success in international dropshipping.

Market Research:

- ***Consumer Preferences:*** Research consumer preferences, buying behaviors, and cultural nuances in each target market.

- ***Competitor Analysis:*** Analyze local competitors to understand the market landscape and identify opportunities.

Localization:

- **Language:** Offer your website and customer support in the local language to enhance customer experience.

- **Marketing:** Tailor your marketing strategies to resonate with local audiences. This includes localized ads, promotions, and content.

Product Selection:

- **Demand**: Choose products that are in demand in your target markets.

- **Seasonality:** Be aware of seasonal variations and local holidays that may affect demand.

6. Legal and Regulatory Considerations

Complying with international laws and regulations is crucial to avoid legal issues and ensure smooth operations.

Intellectual Property:

- **Trademarks and Patents:** Ensure the products you're selling don't infringe on trademarks or patents in your target markets.

- **Brand Protection:** Consider trademarking your brand in key markets to protect your intellectual property.

Consumer Protection Laws:

- *Compliance:* Understand and comply with consumer protection laws in each target market, including return policies, warranties, and advertising standards.

- *Privacy Laws:* Ensure your data handling practices comply with international privacy laws, such as GDPR in Europe.

Taxes and Duties:

- *VAT and GST:* Be aware of VAT, GST, and other sales taxes applicable in your target markets. Consider using services that handle tax calculations and remittances.

- *Customs Duties:* Understand the customs duties that apply to your products and ensure you inform your customers accordingly.

7. Building Relationships with International Suppliers

Strong relationships with your suppliers are essential for a successful dropshipping business. Here's how to build and maintain these relationships:

Communication:

- *Regular Contact:* Maintain regular communication with your suppliers to stay informed about product availability, shipping times, and any potential issues.

- *Clear Expectations:* Clearly communicate your expectations regarding product quality, shipping times, and customer service.

Negotiation:

- *Bulk Orders:* Negotiate better rates and terms for bulk orders or long-term partnerships.

- *Payment Terms:* Discuss payment terms and methods that work best for both parties.

Quality Control:

- *Samples:* Regularly order samples to check product quality and ensure consistency.

- *Feedback Loop:* Provide feedback to suppliers about product quality and customer complaints to facilitate continuous improvement.

Tips for Successful International Dropshipping

Here are some additional tips to help you succeed in international dropshipping:

1. Use Reliable Dropshipping Platforms:

Utilize reliable dropshipping platforms that support international shipping and offer integration with your Shopify store. Platforms like Oberlo, Spocket, and AliExpress Dropshipping are popular choices.

2. Offer Excellent Customer Support:

Provide excellent customer support to address any issues related to international orders. Be proactive in communicating shipping times, customs duties, and other potential concerns. Here's how you can elevate your customer support:

Multilingual Support:

- Language Options: Offer support in multiple languages to cater to your international customers. Use tools like Google Translate for initial interactions if you don't have native speakers.

- Localized Content: Provide FAQs, guides, and help articles in the primary languages of your target markets.

Clear Communication:

- Shipping Updates: Keep customers informed about their order status, including any delays or customs issues.

- Proactive Support: Reach out to customers if there are any issues with their orders before they have to contact you.

Flexible Return Policies:

- Hassle-Free Returns: Make the return process as simple as possible for international customers, considering the potential costs and logistics.

- Local Return Centers: Partner with local warehouses or return centers in key markets to facilitate easier returns.

3. Optimize Your Store for Global Markets:

Tailoring your Shopify store to appeal to an international audience is essential. Here's how to do it:

Localization:

- Language: Translate your website content into the languages of your target markets. Apps like Langify can help with this.

- Currency: Display prices in the local currency of your customers. Shopify has built-in features and apps like Bold Multi-Currency to assist with this.

Design and User Experience:

- Cultural Sensitivity: Be mindful of cultural differences in your design and content. Avoid using images or references that may be inappropriate or offensive in certain cultures.

- Mobile Optimization: Ensure your website is mobile-friendly, as many international customers may shop primarily on their mobile devices.

Payment Methods:

- Local Payment Options: Offer popular local payment methods in addition to global options. For example, offer Alipay for Chinese customers or iDEAL for Dutch customers.

- Secure Payments: Ensure all payment gateways are secure to build trust with international customers.

4. Stay Compliant with International Regulations:

Navigating international regulations can be complex, but it's essential for smooth operations. Here's what you need to focus on:

Tax Compliance:

- VAT and GST: Use Shopify's tax settings or third-party apps to calculate and collect VAT or GST for international orders.

- Customs Duties: Make sure to disclose any potential customs duties and import taxes to your customers at checkout.

Consumer Protection:

- *Return Policies:* Ensure your return policies comply with consumer protection laws in the countries you're selling to.

- *Advertising Standards:* Follow advertising regulations to avoid misleading claims and ensure all marketing content is accurate and truthful.

Privacy Laws:

- *Data Protection:* Comply with data protection laws such as GDPR in Europe. Ensure you have clear privacy policies and obtain necessary customer consents for data processing.

- *Secure Data Handling:* Use secure servers and encryption methods to protect customer data.

5. Monitor and Adapt to Market Trends:

Keeping an eye on market trends can help you stay competitive and adapt to changing consumer behaviors.

Market Research:

- *Trend Analysis:* Use tools like Google Trends, SEMrush, and industry reports to stay updated on trends in your target markets.

- *Competitor Monitoring:* Regularly analyze competitors to understand their strategies and identify opportunities.

Customer Feedback:

- Surveys and Reviews: Gather feedback through surveys and reviews to understand customer preferences and improve your offerings.

- Social Listening: Monitor social media and forums to gauge customer sentiment and identify emerging trends.

Product Adaptation:

- Seasonal Trends: Adjust your product offerings based on seasonal trends and local holidays in different markets.

- New Products: Continuously research and introduce new products that align with the preferences of your international customers.

Conclusion

Expanding your dropshipping business internationally can unlock new growth opportunities and significantly boost your revenue. However, it requires careful planning, a deep understanding of international markets, and the ability to navigate various logistical, legal, and cultural challenges.

By choosing the right countries to dropship from, managing international shipping and customs, adapting your store for global markets, providing excellent customer support, staying compliant with regulations, and monitoring market trends, you can build a successful international dropshipping business.

Remember, every market is unique, and what works in one region may not necessarily work in another. Stay flexible, continually learn from your experiences, and adapt your strategies accordingly. With the right approach and a commitment to excellence, you can thrive in the dynamic world of international dropshipping.

CONCLUSION

As we approach the final chapter of ***"Dropshipping Shopify for Beginners: The All-Inclusive Guide to Establishing and Running a Booming Dropshipping Business "*** I want to seize this opportunity to congratulate you for making it this far.

Your dedication to learning the intricacies of dropshipping and your commitment to building a successful business are commendable. You've absorbed a wealth of knowledge about setting up your store, selecting products, navigating international shipping, and much more. Now, it's time to reflect on your journey and look ahead to the exciting possibilities that await you.

The Journey of Entrepreneurship

Entrepreneurship is a journey filled with highs and lows, challenges and triumphs. Dropshipping, like any other business model, requires perseverance, adaptability, and a willingness to learn continuously. Let's revisit some of the essential lessons and insights you've gained throughout this book.

Embracing the Entrepreneurial Mindset

Success in dropshipping, as in any entrepreneurial endeavor, begins with the right mindset. Here are some key traits and attitudes that will serve you well:

Resilience:

- **Overcoming Obstacles:** Every business faces challenges, whether it's finding reliable suppliers, managing customer expectations, or dealing with logistics. Being resilient enables you to move past setbacks and continue on.

- **Growing from Failures:** See setbacks as chances to improve and gain knowledge. Each mistake brings valuable lessons that can help you improve and avoid similar pitfalls in the future.

Adaptability:

- **Changing Trends:** The e-commerce landscape is dynamic, with new trends and technologies emerging regularly. Being flexible enables you to take advantage of new opportunities and stay ahead of the curve.

- **Customer Feedback:** Listen to your customers and be willing to make changes based on their feedback. This customer-centric approach can lead to better products and services.

Persistence:

- Long-Term Vision: Building a successful dropshipping business takes time and effort. Stay focused on your long-term goals, even when progress seems slow.

- Consistency: Consistent effort and dedication are key to achieving your objectives. Whether it's marketing, customer service, or product sourcing, consistency pays off in the long run.

Key Takeaways from the Book

Throughout this book, we've covered a comprehensive range of topics to equip you with the knowledge and tools you need to succeed in dropshipping. Let's recap some of the most important lessons.

Setting Up Your Shopify Store

Your Shopify store serves as the cornerstone for your dropshipping business. Here's a quick reminder of what you've learned:

Choosing a Niche:

- Finding Your Passion: Select a niche that you're passionate about and that has market demand. This combination helps you stay motivated and connect with your audience.

Design and Usability:

- User-Friendly Design: Ensure your store is easy to navigate, visually appealing, and optimized for mobile devices.

- Professional Branding: Invest in professional branding to create a strong, recognizable identity for your business.

Essential Apps:

- Automation: Use apps to automate tasks like order processing, inventory management, and marketing. This saves time and reduces the chance of mistakes.

- Customer Support: Implement tools for customer support, such as live chat and helpdesk systems, to provide timely assistance to your customers.

Sourcing and Vetting Suppliers:

Reliable suppliers are crucial for delivering quality products and maintaining customer satisfaction. Here are some essential points to always keep in mind:

Finding Suppliers:

- Platforms: Utilize platforms like AliExpress, Oberlo, and Spocket to find potential suppliers.

- Research: Conduct thorough research to vet suppliers, including checking reviews and ordering samples.

Building Relationships:

- **Communication:** Maintain regular communication with your suppliers to build strong relationships and ensure smooth operations.

- **Negotiation:** Don't hesitate to negotiate terms, prices, and shipping methods to benefit your business.

Managing Logistics and Shipping:

Efficient logistics and shipping are vital for customer satisfaction and operational efficiency.

Here's a recap of all you've learned:

Shipping Methods:

- **Options:** Offer multiple shipping options, including standard, expedited, and courier services, to cater to different customer preferences.

- **Tracking:** Always provide tracking information to keep customers informed about their order status.

Customs and Duties:

- Compliance: Understand customs regulations and duties for the countries you're shipping to. Ensure that all relevant documentation is included to avoid delays.

- Transparency: Inform customers about potential customs duties and taxes to avoid surprises and ensure a smooth delivery process.

Marketing and Growing Your Business:

Effective marketing techniques are vital for attracting customers and increasing sales. Let's review some of the important strategies:

Content Marketing:

- *Valuable Content:* Create informative and engaging content, such as blog posts, videos, and guides, to attract and retain customers.

- *SEO:* Optimize your content for search engines to improve visibility and drive organic traffic.

Social Media Marketing:

- *Engagement:* Engagement: Actively interact with your audience on all your social media channels. Share valuable content, respond to comments, and run targeted ad campaigns.

- *Influencer Collaborations:* Partner with influencers in your niche to expand your reach and build credibility.

Email Marketing:

- ***Building a List:*** Grow your email list by offering incentives like discounts and exclusive content.

- ***Personalization:*** Send personalized emails to nurture leads, recover abandoned carts, and promote new products.

Adding Value to Your Business:

To stand out in a competitive market, you need to add value to your business and provide an exceptional customer experience. Here are some strategies to consider:

Unique Value Proposition (UVP):

Your UVP is what sets you apart from competitors and gives customers a compelling reason to buy from you. Ensure your UVP is clear, concise, and communicated effectively across all channels.

Exceptional Customer Service:

Providing excellent customer service helps convert one-time buyers into repeat customers.

Focus on being responsive, helpful, and proactive in addressing customer needs.

High-Quality Products:

Ensuring your products are of high quality can lead to satisfied customers and repeat business. Thoroughly vet your suppliers and regularly order samples to check for consistency.

Example:

- Offer a satisfaction guarantee that allows customers to return products if they're not satisfied with the quality. This shows confidence in your products and builds trust.

Embracing Continuous Learning:

The world of e-commerce is constantly evolving, and continuous learning is essential for staying competitive and adapting to changes. Here's how you can keep learning and growing:

Stay Updated with Industry Trends:

Follow industry blogs, news sites, and podcasts to stay informed about the latest trends and developments. Use tools like Google Trends and SEMrush to identify emerging trends in your niche.

Invest in Education and Training:

Take online courses in e-commerce, digital marketing, and other relevant topics to enhance your skills. Attend webinars and workshops to learn from industry experts and gain practical knowledge.

Experiment and Innovate:

Regularly test new ideas and strategies to see what works best for your business. Stay open to innovative solutions and technologies that can improve your operations and customer experience.

Events and Webinars:

Host events, webinars, or live Q&A sessions to connect with your audience and provide valuable information. Create a private Facebook group or online community for your customers to share tips and connect with each other.

Wishing You Success

As you embark on your journey to becoming a successful dropshipper, I want to wish you the best of luck. The road ahead will have its challenges, but with the knowledge and strategies you've gained from this book, you are well-equipped to navigate them. Remember, success in dropshipping requires persistence, adaptability, and a commitment to continuous learning and improvement.

Believe in yourself and your vision. Stay resilient in the face of obstacles and remain open to learning from every experience. The journey of entrepreneurship is rewarding, filled with opportunities for growth, creativity, and innovation. Embrace it with passion and determination, and you will achieve great success.

Thank you for joining me on this journey through "Dropshipping Shopify for Beginners 2024-2025." I hope this book has provided you with valuable insights and practical advice to help you build and grow your dropshipping business. Here's to your success and the exciting adventures that lie ahead.

Happy Dropshipping!

GLOSSARY OF TERMS

1. Affiliate Marketing: A performance-based marketing strategy where a business rewards affiliates for each customer brought by the affiliate's marketing efforts.

2. AOV (Average Order Value): The average amount of money spent by customers on a single order.

3. B2B (Business to Business): Transactions or business conducted between two businesses.

4. B2C (Business to Consumer): Transactions or business conducted directly between a company and consumers.

5. Backorder: A status given to orders for products that are temporarily out of stock but will be fulfilled once the inventory is replenished.

6. Conversion Rate: The percentage of visitors to an e-commerce site who make a purchase.

7. Cross-Selling: Encouraging customers to purchase additional, related products.

8. Customer Lifetime Value (CLV): The total revenue a business can expect from a single customer over the course of their relationship.

9. Dropshipping: A retail fulfillment method where a store doesn't keep the products it sells in stock. Instead, it purchases the item from a third party and has it shipped directly to the customer.

10. E-commerce Platform: Software applications that allow online businesses to manage their website, sales, and operations.

11. Email Marketing: Using email to promote products or services to potential and current customers.

12. Fulfillment: The complete process of receiving, processing, and delivering orders to customers.

13. Inventory Management: The supervision of non-capitalized assets (inventory) and stock items.

14. Lead Time: The time it takes from receiving an order to delivering the product to the customer.

15. Logistics: The detailed organization and implementation of complex operations, including transportation and storage.

16. Markup: The difference between the cost of a product and its selling price.

17. Merchant Account: A type of bank account that allows businesses to accept payments by debit or credit cards.

18. Niche Market: A specialized segment of the market for a particular kind of product or service.

19. Order Fulfillment: The process of receiving, processing, and delivering orders to customers.

20. Outsource: To contract out a business process or function to a third-party provider.

21. Payment Gateway: A merchant service that authorizes and processes credit card payments for e-commerce transactions.

22. POD (Print on Demand): A process where products are only printed once an order has been made.

23. Profit Margin: The difference between the cost of producing a product and the selling price.

24. Returns Management: The process of managing returned products, including restocking, refurbishing, and resale.

25. SEO (Search Engine Optimization): The practice of increasing the quantity and quality of traffic to a website through organic search engine results.

26. Shopping Cart: An online application that allows customers to accumulate a list of items for purchase.

27. SKU (Stock Keeping Unit): A unique identifier for each distinct product and service that can be purchased.

28. Supply Chain: The network of all the individuals, organizations, resources, activities, and technology involved in the creation and sale of a product.

29. Up-Selling: Encouraging customers to purchase a more expensive item or upgrade.

30. Wholesale: The sale of goods in large quantities, typically to be sold by retailers.

31. *Abandoned Cart:* When a customer adds items to their online shopping cart but leaves the site without completing the purchase.

32. *Chargeback:* A demand by a credit-card provider for a retailer to make good the loss on a fraudulent or disputed transaction.

33. *Customer Acquisition Cost (CAC):* The cost associated with acquiring a new customer, including marketing and sales expenses.

34. *Customer Retention Rate:* The percentage of customers who continue to buy from a business over a given period.

35. *Dropshipper:* A supplier or wholesaler that fulfills orders on behalf of an e-commerce store.

36. *E-Wallet:* A digital wallet that stores payment information and allows users to make electronic transactions.

37. *Fraud Detection:* Techniques and tools used to identify and prevent fraudulent transactions.

38. *Private Label:* Products manufactured by one company for sale under another company's brand.

39. *Product Feed:* A file containing product information, such as prices, descriptions, and images, used for online advertising and marketplaces.

40. User Experience (UX): The overall experience a customer has with a website or application, including usability, design, and functionality.

HOW WAS IT?

Dear Reader,

Thank you for reading "Dropshipping Shopify for Beginners: The All-Inclusive Guide to Establishing and Running a Booming Dropshipping Business." I hope you found the information and strategies within these pages helpful and inspiring as you embark on your dropshipping journey.

Your thoughts and feedback mean the world to me. If you enjoyed the book and found it useful, please consider leaving a rating and review on Amazon. Your support will not only help me improve but also guide other aspiring entrepreneurs to this resource.

Thank you for being a part of this journey. Wishing you great success in your dropshipping business!

Best regards,

T.M.T Harrison